Haynes

Working from
Home
Manual

Kyle MacRae and Gary Marshall

Contents

Introduction

You know that you want to work from home and you believe that you can work from home, but how are you going to convince the boss – or your partner? In this manual, you'll find all the information, advice and tips you could ever need.

Working from home is a fantastic thing and there are lots of benefits – not just for you, but for the rest of the world too. More homeworkers means fewer commuters, which in turn means less congestion and less pollution; for you, it means saving a fortune on travel costs and getting an extra hour or two in bed. For businesses, homeworking enables them to save money on heating, lighting, power and all the other costs of providing office space; for you, it means saving money on everything from work clothes to takeaway sandwiches.

The benefits aren't just financial, though. In a typical office, a lot of your time is spent doing things that aren't directly relevant to your job. You'll spend time answering phone calls for others, or helping colleagues, or waiting for someone else to finish with the printer and, if you're really unlucky, you'll spend an awful lot of time in meetings. When you work from home, those distractions disappear – which means that if you're disciplined, you can use your time much more effectively. Homeworking is also ideal for anyone who can't attend an office every day from nine to five, for example because they've got very young children to look after. The end result: you'll be happier and more productive – and while the rest of the world gets up at the crack of dawn to get ready for work, you'll be nice and toasty in bed.

The internet makes homeworking a lot more social than it used to be: you can communicate with friends and fellow homeworkers via chat software or online discussion forums such as the one at homeworking.com.

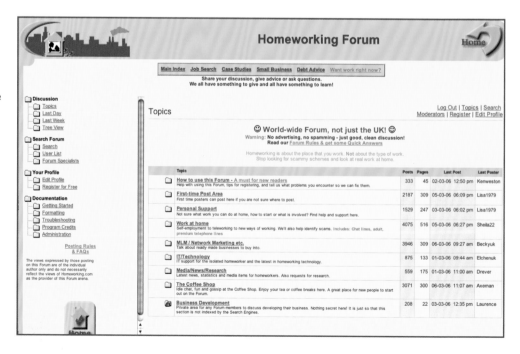

The big question

Before you decide to work from home, you need to answer a very important question: is it the right move for you? Working from home doesn't suit everybody, so it's important to consider the issues carefully.

The biggest single potential problem with working from home is isolation. Although you'll still be in touch with colleagues over the phone and on the occasional visit to the office, it's not the same as going to the office every day – so if the social side of your work is what makes the job worth doing, you might find that homeworking isn't for you.

The other potential problem is focus. With no boss breathing down your neck, you're free to use your time as you choose – which means you need to be very disciplined. If you're easily distracted then the lure of children, pets, relatives or daytime television could prove extremely difficult to resist, and that can cause all kinds of problems. If you're self-employed, if you're playing with the puppy, you're not making money; if you're working for an employer and you don't hit your targets or never seem to be around when the boss phones, you might find that your homeworking career comes to an abrupt end.

That doesn't mean you can't play with the puppy or spend quality time with the kids, of course; being able to do non-work things during the working day is one of the great joys of

homeworking. However, it's important to get the right balance – and when you work from home, finding the right balance between your work and your life is entirely up to you.

How this manual will help

In this manual, we'll cover everything you need to know about working from home. We'll find out how you can set up a fully functioning home office from scratch, how to make the most of limited space and how to make sure everything works together. We'll explore the different hardware and software options, keeping one eye on flexibility and the other on economy. We'll find out how the latest technologies can make your life easier – and, of course, in the usual Haynes style, we'll cut through the jargon and show you how to make the technology work for you.

There's more to working from home than having the right furniture or the right machine, of course. You might be using sensitive data, so we'll take a thorough look at the steps you can take to make sure important information doesn't fall into the wrong hands. We'll help you stay on top of the financial side of things, from the insurance cover you need, to the best ways to make tax less terrifying, and we'll discover the words of wisdom that will help you keep your cool when the lines between your home life and office life have blurred. Most importantly of all, we'll give you all the information you need to ensure that your home office is a place of harmony, not horror!

1

PART

So you want to work from home?

PART ① First things first

Before you start shopping for computers or filing cabinets, it's important to know exactly what you want to achieve, where you want to achieve it and when you're going to do it. If your employer already has a homeworking scheme, you might find that the firm will do all the work and provide all the things you need. In which case, the only thing you need to decide is which room will become your office. However, if you're doing it all yourself then you'll need to plan things carefully.

Location, location, location

Your home is perfect for living in, but it might not be ideal for running a business – particularly if you live in a rural area. For example, while broadband internet connections are available in most of the UK, some parts of the country still can't get it; similarly couriers offer next-day delivery to most of the UK, but more remote regions get a slower delivery service. If broadband or next-day delivery is important to you, then it's a very good idea to check these things before you plan anything else – and it doesn't take long. You can find out broadband availability by checking your phone number on any broadband service provider's website, and you can find out delivery frequencies from courier firms' sites.

If you have the space, an office in the garden can be an ideal solution when areas in the home aren't suitable.

www.thegardenescape.co.uk

Firms such as Econoloft (**www.econoloft.co.uk**) can turn unused loft space into a fully functioning office, but don't forget to speak to your local council's Building Control department first.

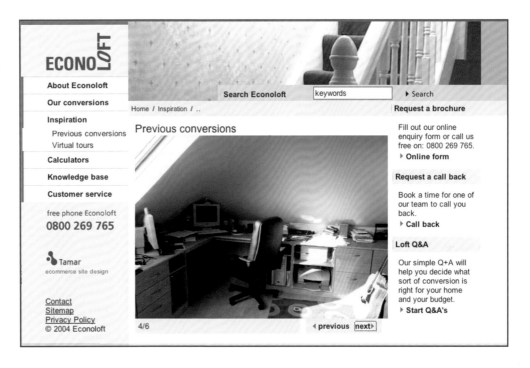

Once you've checked that you can get the services you need, the next step is to decide where in your home you're going to have an office. It's a good idea to have a dedicated room; that way you can close the door at the end of the day and leave the 'office' behind, so you won't be tempted to do a bit more work when you're supposed to be relaxing. It's also handy if you've got pets, because you can use the door to keep them out when you're making important calls, or to stop them from chewing your computer cables. As we'll discover in Appendix 1, if you're self-employed it's good for tax reasons too: it's much easier to claim a proportion of your heating and electricity bills if your office isn't also the guest bedroom.

What happens if you want an entire room but don't have a spare one? There's always the shed: the Sunday supplements regularly feature adverts from firms who can convert a shed or garage into a home office, or who will build one from scratch at the back of your garden. As you'd expect, it's not cheap – and you might need to get planning permission from the council. Some houses have large loft spaces that can be converted; however, once again there's a hefty cost involved and you'll need to liaise with the council.

If you don't have a spare room and don't fancy converting the shed, don't despair: there's no reason why you can't simply use a spare corner somewhere. However, if at all possible, it's a good idea to make your work area separate from your living area, so for example if you use a corner of the dining room for your office

then you could use screens or other furniture to block the area off from the rest of the room.

There's no such thing as the perfect place for a home office – it's whatever suits your available space and your way of working. However, no matter where you decide to work, take the following issues into account.

Light and heat

There should be enough light for you to get your job done without eye strain, and ideally that light should be natural – it makes your working environment much more pleasant. Beware of glare, particularly if you have a traditional CRT computer monitor which uses reflective glass. Flat-panel monitors don't suffer as badly from glare, but if you already own a CRT screen then a set of window blinds might be cheaper than a new monitor and just as effective.

Ideally, your working area should also have heating and a window you can open – particularly in summer, when a small office can easily become a sauna. In winter you'll definitely feel the cold, particularly if you've spent all day being relatively inactive and working on a computer, so make sure you can bring your work area to a reasonable temperature unless you fancy typing while wearing mittens. A small desktop fan can be a big help too, especially if you're using a CRT monitor in an enclosed space: such monitors generate a surprising amount of heat.

Space

Think about what you need to have nearby: in addition to a decent-sized desk and a chair, you'll need room for your phone and whatever you're working on. You'll probably need storage, too, either in the form of filing cabinets or shelving, and if you think you'll have people visiting while you work then you'll need room for them to sit.

With careful planning and carefully chosen furniture you can get a surprising amount of stuff into a narrow space – we're writing this in a converted cupboard just a few feet square, but we've managed to cram three computers, two phones, a printer, a bookcase, a small filing cabinet and a full-sized desk and chair into it – but it's important to make sure in advance. There's nothing more annoying than discovering that your shiny new desk is an inch too wide for the office. However, too much space can be as much of a problem as too little: you'll find that your working area will inevitably expand to fill the available space, so if you'll be using a large space then it's a good idea to be disciplined about how much of it you use.

In most cases, you'll need room for more than just your screen, your keyboard and your mouse. If you're working in graphic design you'll need space for a graphics tablet, and in most types of work you'll have to deal with paperwork as well as computer work – so make sure there'll be enough room for you to fill out forms or scribble notes when you're not typing.

It's also a good idea to look at the layout of your house before investing in furniture, particularly ready-assembled furniture. Staircases and narrow hallways can make it difficult or impossible to get ready-assembled furniture from the front door to your office, so flat-packed furniture would make setting up your office much easier.

Power and phones

Your chosen space should have sufficient electrical sockets for the amount of equipment you intend to use: endless extension leads can overload your sockets, be a trip hazard, and be a tempting target when a pet's looking for something to chew. You'll need a phone point within easy reach, too: cheap phone extension cables can reduce the quality of the phone signal, which can reduce the performance of your internet connection. It's a good idea to have a proper phone point in your work area rather than running extension leads across the house.

Shared spaces

If you can't turn an entire room into an office, think carefully about what room you'll be using. A spare bedroom could be ideal, but it does mean you won't be able to work if you have guests staying over. A downstairs room isn't ideal if you have children running around (unless, of course, you want to be able to keep an eye on the kids while you're working and don't mind a soundtrack of cartoons or crying when you're on the phone). If you live alone then you don't need to worry about interruptions

Working in the dining room is fine, but screening off an area will help to separate work and home life.

Safety should always be your number one priority. Fit smoke alarms if you don't already have them and make sure you have a first aid kit within easy reach.

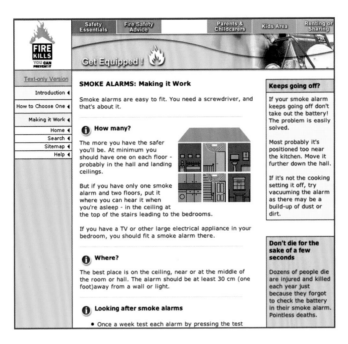

and you can work anywhere you wish, but if you share your home with adults, children or animals then you should try and find a work area where you won't be interrupted by the everyday hustle and bustle of living.

Safety and security

If possible, make sure your equipment can't be seen from the street: it could be an open invitation to burglars. If you can't find a suitable working location that doesn't display your expensive equipment, make sure you have strong doors and windows with sturdy locks, and consider an alarm system too (these things are a good idea for any home, but if your computers can be seen from the street then they're essential). Blinds can make it harder for people to see in, and some workstation furniture can be folded shut at the end of the working day so that it just looks like a cupboard – which has the extra bonus of hiding your clutter as well as your hardware!

If you share your home with young children or pets, is there a danger that a curious hand or paw might bring your entire computer setup crashing to the ground? You can restrict access by using baby gates or by locking doors, although of course that's not an option if you're using a corner of the dining room. If you are, once again it may be worth considering fold-away furniture that puts your office out of the kids' or pets' reach when you're not there.

Don't forget the essentials, either: you'll need a smoke alarm and a first aid kit, and if you have a serious medical condition it's a very good idea to ask a friend or relative to contact you regularly to make sure you're all right. If your condition flares up when you're in an office, there are plenty of people around who can call for help on your behalf, but when you work from home, you're on your own.

PART 1

The shopping list

Once you've identified where you're going to put your office, you can start finding things to put in it. No two offices are the same, but for a typical home office you'll need some or all of the following items.

A decent desk and chair

A good quality desk and chair aren't just important: they're essential. However, we often have a strange attitude to work equipment: while many people will happily spend more than £1,000 on a sofa, they'll balk at paying more than £50 for a desk and chair. When you think about it, that doesn't make sense: you're on the sofa for an hour or two per day, but you're sitting on your work chair for eight hours a day.

There's nothing wrong with a cheap desk and chair if you'll only be using it for very short periods of time, but when you're using it all day every day then it makes sense to go for something that's designed for long-term use. That doesn't mean you need to spend hundreds of pounds on a masterpiece of industrial design, but if you're going to be using a computer then look for a desk that's up to the job. It should be big enough not just for your computer, but also for your paperwork, mouse, phone and other essential items, and it should have a lowered tray for your computer keyboard (even if you're planning to use a laptop computer).

The Herman Miller Aeron chair is the Rolls-Royce of office furniture, but you don't need to spend several hundred pounds for a good quality chair. Make sure that your chosen chair is designed for office work – a dining room chair won't do!

The chair is even more important than your desk: a bad chair will encourage bad posture, which can lead to backache and increase the risk of unpleasant ailments such as repetitive strain injury (RSI). See Appendix 3 for more information on how computers can seriously damage your health. A good chair should be adjustable in height, should adequately support your back, and should have a large enough seating area to support your bottom and thighs. Chairs come in different sizes, so it's a good idea to try several different ones before you make a final choice.

When you're thinking about office furniture, don't forget about flooring: heavy chairs with castors will quickly destroy domestic carpets, so it might be a good idea to invest in plastic carpet protectors or a heavyweight rug. If you have wooden or laminate floors, heavy chairs can cause scratching – and if you have downstairs neighbours, the noisy combination of a heavy chair and a wooden floor could make you very unpopular.

Somewhere to put your stuff

So much for the paperless office: no matter what kind of work you do, you'll end up having to store stacks of paper. You'll need to store letters and contracts or other business correspondence, receipts, computer manuals, telephone directories, software boxes and so on, and if your job involves a lot of customer paperwork you'll need somewhere to store that too. There's no right way to store things: some people use filing cabinets, while others prefer to put things in lever arch files and stick them on shelves or in a bookcase. It doesn't matter which you go for, but when you're planning your office remember to allow space for it.

You'll also need somewhere to store discs such as software CDs, backup discs, printer drivers and so on. We'd recommend a small disc storage wallet or box, which you can get for a few pounds from a local supermarket. These take up very little space and ensure that your discs won't get scratched or exposed to sunlight, but be careful where you put them: if you use a CD wallet and leave it on a windowsill during a sunny day, you might find that the heat melts the CD labels and turns them into a sticky mess.

Computer and telephone equipment

You'll need a desktop or laptop computer, a printer (or a multifunction device that prints, copies and scans documents) and other necessary computer hardware, a broadband connection, a phone and possibly a fax too. We'll look at the various options in Part 2.

Other bits and bobs

A good desk lamp makes life easier, not just in winter or at night but also when you're poring over small print in documents. You'll need the usual office supplies such as printer paper, notepads, pens, envelopes and post-it notes. If you plan to back up your computer files (a very good idea) you'll need blank CD-R discs, or an external hard disk if you intend to back up a lot of files at

high speed. If you're self-employed, you might want professionally printed headed paper and business cards too.

All of these items cost money, and they might involve long delivery times – and don't forget that you'll need to order services such as a new broadband connection or telephone line too. Assume that at least one thing will take longer than advertised and you're unlikely to be disappointed: for example, getting broadband for our office should have taken three days but, thanks to various mistakes by our service provider, it took two months before we were up and running. If something's going to be essential to your work, order it as early as you possibly can. It's better to have boxes cluttering up your house for a few weeks than to try to work without a broadband connection or a phone line.

It's a very good idea to redecorate your work area before you start using it, too: it's much easier to paint or wallpaper your working area when it's empty than when it's full of equipment and you've got deadlines to meet.

By now you should have a clear idea of where you're going to work, when you're going to start, and what you need to get the job done. The next step is to start choosing the specific tools you're going to use – and, in Part 2, that's exactly what we'll do.

if you need to get a new telephone line or broadband, allow plenty of extra time so they're in place when you start homeworking.

2

PART  # Choosing the right hardware

The most important part of your home office is likely to be your computer. It's where you'll do the majority of your work, it's where you'll probably keep track of your finances, and it's likely to be the main way in which you communicate with colleagues or clients. There's a huge range of machines to choose from, ranging from cheap and cheerful machines to state-of-the-art – and ultra-expensive – systems. If your employer provides your equipment then the choice will already be made for you, but if you're selecting your own equipment then don't let the sheer amount of choice put you off. Finding the right machine is easier than you might think.

There's no such thing as a one-size-fits-all computer: manufacturers make different machines for different markets. For example, the cheapest machines are perfectly capable of carrying out everyday tasks such as word processing, browsing the internet or sending and receiving email, but they'll struggle with more complex jobs such as photo editing or video editing. They'll also struggle with the latest games, so if you want to get a PC that you can use for fun as well as for work then it's a good idea to avoid the bargain basement models.

PART

PC versus Mac

Every day, arguments rage across the internet between fans of PCs and fans of Apple Macs. Mac fans look down on PC owners because they think Macs are superior machines; PC fans look down on Mac owners because they think PCs offer better value for money.

So is there any real difference between a Mac and a PC? Yes, but the differences aren't as big as they used to be. For example, the cheapest Mac used to be just under £1,000 while the cheapest PCs were under £400. That's changed and you can pick up a basic Mac Mini for £449. Another change is that Macs no longer use different processors to PCs: Macs use Intel chips, just like most PCs do.

There's one major difference between Macs and PCs, though: PCs usually run Windows and Macs run an operating system called OS X. Crucially, OS X isn't compatible with Windows; that means that Windows programs won't run on a Mac, and Mac programs won't run on a PC – although if you have the right software, you can share files between the two kinds of systems. Many programs are available for both platforms, so for example Microsoft makes a version of Office for the Mac as well as Office for Windows; Adobe makes versions of Photoshop for both platforms; and big-name programs such as the web design giant, Dreamweaver, are available for both PCs and Macs too.

Although the really famous programs tend to be available in Mac and PC versions, you'll find that an awful lot of programs are PC-only. It may still be possible to run them on a Mac via

Desktop PCs are the cheapest and most flexible kinds of computers, although of course you can't take them with you when you travel or attend client meetings.

Apple's free Boot Camp software enables you to install and run a full copy of Windows XP on a Mac, but you'll need to buy a copy of Windows – and Apple won't provide technical support if you encounter problems.

Virtual PC software, which essentially creates a fake PC inside your Mac, but such software is very slow, costs extra and isn't compatible with 100% of PC programs (and at the time of writing, it doesn't work on the latest, Intel-powered Macs). If you need to run the same software as your employer or client, you might find that it makes your life easier if you choose the same kind of computer that they use.

Virtual PC isn't the only way to run Windows programs on a Mac, though. If you have an Intel-powered Mac, you can now install and run Windows XP using a program called Boot Camp (which you can download for free from **www.apple.com/macosx/bootcamp**). This enables you to install a full copy of Windows XP on your Mac, and it adds a startup menu to the system that enables you to choose between Windows and OS X when you switch your machine on. Unlike Virtual PC, when you run Windows via Boot Camp it's just as fast as running Windows on a PC.

Boot Camp essentially gives you two machines for the price of one, but there are some potential issues too. Apple doesn't provide any technical support for Windows, so if something goes wrong you're on your own, and Boot Camp doesn't include a copy of Windows – so you'll need to buy one. At the time of writing, that means paying £177 for a copy of Windows XP Home Edition or £286 for Windows XP Professional.

Another factor that might influence your choice is whether you intend to use other gadgets, such as a Pocket PC computer or a smartphone. Such devices are very handy; they enable you to synchronise your diary between phone and PC or check your email when you're on the move. However, some devices work with both PCs and Macs, but others are Windows-only. For example, most Pocket PCs and Windows Mobile-powered smartphones are designed specifically to work with PCs, and while it's often possible to make them work with Macs, you'll usually need additional software – and you won't be able to call technical support if you encounter a problem.

You might encounter similar issues with other devices, such as multi-function printers, plug-in cards that enable your laptop to access the net via your mobile phone connection and so on. While many such machines work happily with any computer, some are PC-only – which means it's essential to think about the big picture when you're weighing up the pros and cons of a PC and a Mac.

There's a third kind of computer, too: a PC running Linux, a free alternative to Windows. It's not something you need to worry about when deciding whether to get a PC or a Mac – PCs that can run Windows can generally run Linux too – but we'll take a good look at Linux in Part 3 of this manual.

Like all laptops, Apple's MacBook Pro enables you to work from almost anywhere. However, convenience costs: laptops are significantly more expensive than the equivalent desktop computers.

Desktop versus laptop

Once you've decided between a PC and a Mac, the next decision is between a desktop and a laptop. Laptops are portable and desktops aren't, but there are other key differences between the two kinds of machines. If you need to work in several different locations then a laptop is likely to be the best machine for you, but if you don't need portability then a desktop is usually the better bet. You should consider the following main issues.

Price

Laptop computers have plummeted in price over the last few years, but you'll still pay a big premium for portability. That's because laptop components are made in lower volumes than desktop ones, and they need to be specially designed for toughness and power efficiency. Inevitably, that comes at a cost, so expect to pay roughly 40% more for a laptop than a similarly specified desktop.

The difference can be even bigger when you're buying the very fastest machines. For example, at the time of writing one big-name PC manufacturer offers two very fast machines: a 'mega multimedia monster' desktop PC and an 'extreme gaming' notebook. The desktop is around £1,000, and the laptop £2,000 – but the desktop outperforms the notebook in several key areas. The processor is faster – a 3GHz dual-core chip compared to the laptop's 2.6GHz single-core processor – and the hard disk is bigger too (320GB compared to 100GB). Unsurprisingly, the desktop has a bigger screen as well: a 19-inch flat-panel monitor compared to the laptop's 17-inch screen.

That doesn't mean you can't buy a cheap laptop: you can get a machine with an Intel Celeron processor for less than £400. However, the price difference still applies. The same manufacturer whose high-end machines we've just looked at also offers bargain-basement computers, and its cheapest laptop is £339. Its cheapest desktop, though, is £279 – and it has twice the memory, twice the disk space and almost twice the processing speed.

Speed

The faster a PC's processor, the more power it needs – and the more power a laptop needs, the bigger the drain on its battery. That means every laptop has to find a compromise between power and battery life, but desktops don't have such worries – so the very fastest computers are all desktops. However, it's important to keep speed in perspective: if you're going to be browsing the internet or writing documents, any computer will be fast enough: the weak links are the speed of your internet connection (or of the site you're visiting) in the first case, and your typing speed in the second.

Memory

Laptop memory tends to be much more expensive than desktop memory and laptops have fewer memory slots – so upgrading a desktop PC with extra RAM will be much cheaper than upgrading a laptop. If you're buying a laptop, get as much memory as you can when you order it: a memory upgrade that adds £100 to the purchase price will save you several times that amount if you leave the upgrade until later. The same applies to all-in-one PCs such as Apple's iMac, which manages to hide an entire computer behind the LCD screen: such machines are much better looking and more compact than traditional desktops, but they're not as easy or as cheap to upgrade.

Disk space

At the time of writing, desktop PCs with 300GB hard disks are everywhere – but most laptop hard disks are 80GB. Once again that's due to the trade-off between power, portability and energy efficiency: 300GB hard disks are currently far too bulky and power-hungry to fit inside a laptop case. It's a similar story with optical media such as DVD drives or CD burners: the ones in desktop machines are typically much faster than the ones in laptops, and it's usually difficult and expensive to upgrade such drives in laptop computers.

Screen size

The bigger the screen, the heavier – and the more expensive – a laptop becomes. Screens also place huge demands on a laptop's battery, which means that in many cases less is more: a machine with a 12 inch screen will usually get better battery life than one with a 17 inch screen. However, most laptops can be connected to an external monitor when you're in the office, and some of them can run dual-screen setups – so you can have the laptop screen showing one program, and a separate, external monitor showing a different program.

Connections

A typical desktop PC has plenty of room in its case, which means manufacturers can put lots of connectors into it. For example you might have four, six or even eight USB ports, a network port, a modem port, a keyboard and mouse connector, a joystick port, three sockets for hooking up surround sound speakers and so on; on a laptop you'll typically get a couple of USB ports, a network port, a modem port and a headphone socket. Most laptops also include a PC Card slot, which enables you to add credit card-sized add-ons such as wireless network cards or other peripherals, but such cards are often very expensive.

Upgradeability

The golden rule of upgrading laptops is usually 'don't bother': by all means add extra, external devices via USB ports, but you'll find that opening up the case and replacing core components is difficult (if not impossible) and, in many cases, incredibly expensive.

Let's look at an example, an Apple Powerbook G4 with a 15 inch screen. Adding 1GB of memory costs £340 and upgrading the hard disk to a speedier version is around £100. However, the company that sells the hard disk upgrades warns that 'user installation is advised against'. As it explains, the machine's hard drive 'is very difficult to get to, and is not classified by Apple as a user installable part. Installing a replacement drive during warranty will void any remaining warranty … we cannot offer instructions or support for the install'. In other words, Apple says it's a bad idea, the firm offering the upgrades says it's a bad idea, and if you muck it up and damage your machine in the process then tough luck.

Size

Yes, we're stating the obvious: unless you buy a very small PC (more about them in a moment), desktop computers are much bigger than laptop ones. However, it's something you should still think about, because if you're short of space in your home office then a laptop might be a better buy than a desktop that dominates the room.

Portability

In 2005, sales of laptop computers overtook sales of desktops – but we're willing to wager that the majority of those laptops have never moved from their owners' desks. If you need a computer that you can take anywhere, for example, so you can pitch ideas to potential or existing clients, then a laptop is the only sensible choice. However, before you pay the premium for portability it's worth thinking about whether you really need a portable PC.

It's true that you can use laptops on trains or planes, but how often do you travel – and how often do you need to work when you're travelling? It's also true that wireless-enabled laptops enable you to access the internet when you're on the move, but modern smartphones can do the same for a lot less cash. And if you're considering a laptop because it will enable you to watch DVDs on long journeys, it's worth remembering that you can buy a portable DVD player for less than £100 – and it's likely to have better battery life to boot. And don't forget that even the most portable laptops are still heavy; the novelty of carrying a dead weight on your shoulders so you can play Solitaire in the airport soon wears off!

Remember, too, that laptops are fragile. Rather than spend thousands on a state-of-the-art laptop it might make more sense to split your money and buy a cheap laptop and a decent desktop. That way you get all the benefits of a portable computer, but if you accidentally drop it you won't have lost your only machine – and you won't have to pay a fortune to replace it.

The latest laptops – such as Toshiba's Qosmio range – are very powerful, but they do mean you'll be carrying a very expensive computer on your travels. It's often sensible to buy a basic laptop for travelling.

PART  What about a mini PC?

In addition to desktops and laptop computers, there's a third option: the mini PC. The most high-profile example is Apple's Mac Mini, but a range of PC manufacturers offer Windows-powered equivalents. Although each machine is different, mini PCs manage to cram an entire desktop computer into a case that's roughly the size of a large book.

There are lots of reasons to like mini PCs. They're incredibly small and usually very quiet, and they manage to pack a decent amount of power into their tiny cases – although the cheapest ones tend to deliver adequate, rather than spectacular, performance. There are other are drawbacks too. The small case means that upgrading a mini PC is usually as difficult and as expensive as upgrading a laptop, and there's no room for add-on cards such as the ones you can put in a traditional desktop computer. As with laptops you can add additional devices such as external hard disks via USB, but we think that rather defeats the point of buying a tiny computer in the first place.

There's no doubt that mini PCs such as Apple's Mac Mini pack a lot of power into a tiny space, but the purchase price doesn't include a monitor, a keyboard or a mouse. Upgrading mini PCs can be expensive, too.

PART

What about a tablet PC?

Tablet PCs are strange beasts: at first they look like normal Windows-powered laptops, but if you swivel the screen around they become electronic notepads. That means you can use them to scribble notes or create drawings, and you can use them with a stylus instead of a keyboard. They can even turn your handwriting into computer-readable text, so for example you could scribble notes in a meeting and get the Tablet PC to turn your notes into a Word document.

According to Microsoft, the firm that came up with the idea of Tablet PCs, such devices are the 'evolution of notebook computing'. It's certainly an impressive technology, but unfortunately it does suffer from a fairly major problem: price. Tablet PCs are more complicated to make than normal laptops, and as a result they cost quite a lot more. For example, at the time of writing the cheapest Tablet PC at **dabs.com** is £892.98; a similarly specified laptop is £428. There's also a much smaller selection to choose from: dabs.com sells ten different Tablet PCs, but 246 different laptops.

Tablet PCs are very impressive: one moment they're laptops, the next minute they're electronic easels that can turn your handwriting into Word documents or annotate images.

Inspect a gadget

Technology firms have become adept at cramming huge amounts of power into ever-decreasing amounts of space, and it's quite possible to buy a handheld computer with more processing power than a desktop PC of just a few years back. That's particularly handy for homeworkers who need to make the occasional business trip: instead of lugging a laptop around, you can take a handheld PC or smartphone with you instead. Such devices typically come in three flavours: ultramobile PCs, PDAs, and smartphones.

Ultramobile PCs

Ultramobile PCs aren't the same as ultraportable PCs, which are just lightweight laptops: at the time of writing, the only ultramobile PCs come from a firm called OQO (**www.oqo.com**), which makes the Ultra Personal Computer. It's a fully-fledged Windows XP computer that includes a keyboard and a screen, but it's just 4.9 inches wide, 3.4 inches high and 0.9 inches deep.

As we've already discovered, portability comes at a price – and in the case of the OQO, it's a hefty one. The OQO costs around £1,500, its keyboard is tiny, and its 1GHz processor is slow compared to even a budget laptop. According to *PC Plus* magazine, it's 'an awesome achievement [but] in practice it's almost entirely pointless': while it's an impressive feat of engineering, 'it's hard to imagine a usage model for which a 10-inch ultraportable notebook PC with a sensible keyboard wouldn't be a far better bet'.

PDAs

Personal Digital Assistants – PDAs – come in two forms: standalone handheld computers and PDAs that double as mobile phones. Such devices are much bigger than phones – although the very latest Windows Mobile machines are less brick-like than most – and they're designed to supplement rather than replace traditional computers.

In the same way that you can choose between PCs and Macs, there are different kinds of PDAs. The most common models are Pocket PCs, which run a stripped-down version of Windows and which are designed to work with Windows PCs (you can make them work with Macs, but you'll need extra software that works with some, but not all, models) but if you're planning to use a Mac, then a Palm-powered PDA will work better.

The idea behind a PDA is that you can take data from your PC when you're out and about, and when you return you connect it to the PC and upload any changes. For example, you can take your calendar and contacts book with you and make changes on your PDA; when you get back to the office, the PDA updates your PC.

The OQO ultraportable PC crams an entire Windows XP computer into a package the size of a paperback book, but it's not as powerful as a full-size laptop computer.

PDAs such as HP's iPaq enable you to take your calendar, contacts book and important files with you when you're out and about. Some models work with wireless networks, too.

PDAs can do more than just keep track of calendars and contacts, though. They can read and edit documents or spreadsheets, you can use them as digital voice recorders, and some of them include wireless networking so you can access the internet – including corporate networks – or check your email on the move (provided you have an account with a wireless service provider such as BTOpenZone). Even the ones without such connections can connect to the internet by establishing a wireless infra-red connection or Bluetooth connection with your mobile.

Smartphones

Until recently, phones were phones and PDAs were PDAs. However, the lines have begun to blur: O_2's XDA phones are Pocket PCs that double as mobile phones, Orange's SDA phones are phones that include most of the features of a Pocket PC, and the Blackberry – which is available from most mobile operators – is a mobile phone that's also designed to deliver email on the move.

As the technology improves, the lines are getting even blurrier. For example, O_2's XDA Mini S, XDA IIs and XDA Exec have keyboards (albeit small ones) that enable you to type entire documents – although we wouldn't recommend doing so for long periods, as the keyboards are fairly awkward to use – and they include wireless network support for mobile internet access. They can be cheap, too: while a decent Pocket PC can cost around £400, a similarly specified smartphone can be less than £80 or even free if you also take out a 12-month mobile phone contract.

Inevitably, compromises are involved. Pocket PCs that double as mobile phones are much bigger and heavier than normal phones, and you might feel daft holding one up to your ear; phone-sized Pocket PCs can be fiddly to navigate, especially if they don't have a touch screen or keyboard like their bigger brothers. Battery life suffers, too: while normal mobile phones offer several hours of talk time and several days on standby, if you use a phone as a PDA then you should expect to recharge it every day – or more often if you use wireless networking or Bluetooth connections, which make big demands on the battery. If your chosen model uses a stylus, you'll also need to get used to ordering more: like odd socks and biros, styli have an amazing ability to vanish, never to be seen again. However, smartphones are a useful alternative to a laptop if you only need to read the odd document, check the odd email or quickly browse the internet when you're out and about and don't fancy carrying a PDA and a phone at the same time.

The lines between PDAs and phones are becoming blurry: for example, O_2's XDA Exec is a phone, but it's also a Pocket PC with a full keyboard and wireless network support.

Prints charming

A computer isn't the only piece of equipment you'll need. Most of us need to print out documents, which means you need a printer; you might also need to scan documents or images, take photocopies or send and receive faxes. You don't necessarily need a different machine for each job, though. Some multi-function printers don't just print, but scan, copy and fax too, and when you're setting up a home office they're more economical than buying a separate machine for each job.

The majority of multi-function printers print, scan and copy, but not all of them include fax features – and you might not need them, because any PC or Mac with a modem can also send and receive faxes. However, a fax machine comes into its own when you need to send things that aren't already on your computer. Using a computer fax means you'd first have to scan the documents into your PC before sending them; with a normal fax or a multi-function printer, it's just a matter of putting the document in the machine and hitting the send button. And of course, a fax machine can receive faxes even when your computer's switched off, or when you've taken your laptop to a meeting.

Alternatively you could use a fax-to-email service, which as the name suggests, receives faxes and emails them to you. Such services give you a dedicated fax number that receives your faxes, turns them into images and sends them to your email account. Fax-to-email services are reasonably cheap – for example, Yac Fax (**www.yac.com**) is £6 per month – and are particularly useful if you work from various different sites: you can access your faxes from anywhere that you can get access to the internet.

Fax or no fax, if you're thinking about a multifunction printer there are several key points you might want to consider – and the big one is whether you should get an inkjet printer or a laser one.

Inkjet versus laser

Printers use one of two technologies: inkjet, where tiny nozzles spray the paper with microscopic drops of ink, and lasers, which use static electricity and heated rollers to bond black or coloured dust to the page. Laser printers are generally best suited to high volume printing, but inkjets are better for printing photographs and are usually cheaper to buy.

No matter what kind of printer you're considering, it's important to remember that printers are sold in the same way as razor blades: you get the razor cheap, but the manufacturer makes its money from selling replacement blades. It's exactly the same with ink cartridges (for inkjets) or toner cartridges (for lasers): the cheaper the printer, the less economical it's likely to be in the long run.

When you're looking at the long-term cost of a printer, check the price and page yield (how many pages you should expect between replacements) of replacement ink or toner cartridges. If you think you'll be doing a lot of colour printing, make sure your potential purchase can use high-volume cartridges – most do – as these will save you lots of money in the long run. Make sure you compare like with like, though: while most manufacturers' page yield figures are based on 5% page coverage – that is, 5% of the page surface is covered in ink or toner – for black printing, some firms base their colour figures on 15% coverage while others stick with 5%. For example HP quotes a page yield of 350 pages from a colour cartridge for the Photosmart 3210 printer, but that's based on 15% coverage; Canon quotes an average of 490 pages for the MP500 printer, but that's based on 5% coverage.

If you're thinking about an inkjet printer, remember to factor in the cost of paper. Lasers will produce great results on even poor quality paper, but if you intend to print photographs with an inkjet then normal copy paper isn't up to the job. It's too porous, so the ink saturates the paper and makes it go curly. For best results you'll need specially coated inkjet paper which, you won't be surprised to read, costs considerably more than copy paper. For example, stationers Rymans sells 500 sheets of good quality copy paper for £3.49, or 0.6p per sheet; a 20-pack of premium photo paper – which, to be fair, is one of the most expensive kinds of inkjet paper – for an HP inkjet is £13.99, or 69.9p per sheet.

With lasers, look at the life expectancy of drums as well as toner cartridges: the drums need replacing too, and they cost between £50 and £100. Depending on the printer, you may need to replace the drum after 12,000 to 20,000 pages, although some manufacturers combine toner and drums in a single package which needs to be replaced more often.

To get the best results from an inkjet printer, you'll need to use specially designed paper. Photo printing is particularly pricey, as it requires heavyweight gloss or matte papers.

Watch the numbers

Multi-function printers are usually described using figures, and the most important ones (other than the price, of course) are print speed and scanning resolution. Unfortunately, printer manufacturers are like car manufacturers: in much the same way that you'll never achieve your car's top speed or quoted fuel consumption, printers don't print as fast as the figures suggest and they can't always scan at the quoted resolution.

While a 32ppm printer can indeed print at 32 pages per minute, that speed is for black and white printing in draft mode; printing in high quality mode slows things down considerably. Colour printing is even more complicated and as a result, takes longer – particularly at the highest quality settings.

Scanning resolution is expressed in dots per inch; the higher the number, the better quality the scans. However, the figures can be misleading: for example, Lexmark offers a multi-function printer with a scanning resolution of 19,200 dots per inch, but the optical resolution is much lower: 1,200 by 2,400 dots per inch. The optical resolution is the important bit, because that's how many dots the scanner can actually see; the higher figure is achieved by using software, which attempts to make a scan look higher resolution than it actually is. You've probably encountered a similar thing with digital cameras: the optical zoom enables you to get closer to an image without losing image quality, but when you switch to digital zoom things become unpredictable. When you're comparing different machines, always compare the optical resolution rather than the sexy, 'enhanced' figure.

Finally, look for the figures for a printer's duty cycle. This tells you how many pages per month the printer is designed to handle, so if you think you'll be churning out several forests per week then look for a machine that can comfortably handle such volumes. If your printer packs up because you've been using it for more printing than it's designed to handle, you'll usually find that the warranty is no longer valid.

Multi-function devices are ideal for homeworkers, because they replace several machines. A single multi-function printer doesn't just print: it scans and photocopies too. Some models even include a fax machine.

Laser printers tend to be designed for high-volume printing. They're slightly more expensive to buy than inkjets, but they're often more economical to run.

Talk is cheap

No home office is complete without a telephone, but the choice isn't just between getting a BT phone line or one from a competitor. You could use a mobile phone or a hybrid phone, which acts as a mobile when you're out and about and like a traditional phone when you're in the office – or you could use a new technology called Voice over IP (VoIP), which uses the internet to massively cut the cost of calling. So which one should you choose?

Traditional phones

If you've already got a standard phone line, don't use it for business: you should be able to differentiate between personal calls and business ones (especially if you're self-employed and claiming the cost of calls against tax), and the last thing you need is a business call interrupting you when you're not working – or a crucial contact being unable to reach you because the kids are chatting to their friends. It's easy and relatively cheap to get a second line installed and you'll get a separate number you can give your business contacts. There's also a huge range of phones to choose from, ranging from cheap and cheerful models to state-of-the-art cordless wonders. Remember, though, that cordless phones need a power supply in order to operate – so you can't use them to make emergency calls during a power cut.

Even if you decide not to go for a standard phone, you might still need a standard phone line: you can't get ADSL broadband without one. However, it doesn't have to be a BT line. Firms such as Bulldog Broadband can provide you with a phone line, and instead of receiving bills from BT you'll be billed by Bulldog. Cable firms such as NTL provide phone services too, and you can get a package that delivers cable broadband, a phone and digital TV for one monthly payment.

Mobile phones

The big advantage of a mobile phone is that you can take it anywhere you go, but there's a big downside: the cost of calls. While all the mobile networks offer package deals, such as 200 minutes of free calls, the cost of calling from a mobile phone is much higher than the cost of calling from a normal phone. If a company isn't paying the bills, it's a good idea to limit the use of your mobile to when you're out of the office.

As with a normal phone, if you're claiming the cost of calls against tax you should only use your mobile for business.

If you think you'll be travelling abroad and plan to use a mobile, look very carefully at roaming rates. Roaming rates are the costs of calling from foreign countries using your mobile, and they can vary dramatically between network operators. Roaming charges apply not just for making calls, but for receiving them and for sending text messages too, and they can be hefty: we recently spent three days in the USA and managed to rack up a phone bill of £280!

BT's new Fusion service is a mobile phone when you're out and about, but when you return to the office it uses your wireless network to make cheaper calls.

Hybrid phones

Hybrid phones, such as BT's Fusion, aim to give you the best of both worlds: when you're out and about they're normal mobile phones, but when you're back in the office you pay landline, not mobile, rates. The Fusion works via wireless networking and broadband, so when you're in the office it uses your wireless network to make calls via the internet. It's very clever and can save you a lot of money, but of course it's useless without a broadband internet connection and a wireless network.

Internet phones

One of the most exciting new communications technologies is Voice over IP, or VoIP for short. Instead of using the telephone network to make calls, it sends your voice over the internet – which means if the person you're calling is also using VoIP, the call won't cost you a penny. If you've ever used voice chat on a computer, it works in exactly the same way.

The best known internet phone system is Skype (**www.skype.com**), which was originally designed as a PC service: to use it you'd plug a headset into your computer. However, you can now buy Skype-compatible phones that plug directly into your broadband connection, bypassing your PC altogether, and there are even cordless models: the base station plugs into your broadband connection, and you can use the phone anywhere that's within broadcast range. You can also call people who don't have Skype, using the SkypeOut service: this enables Skype users to call any telephone number in the world, at rates that are usually much lower than traditional phone companies' rates.

Skype isn't the only VoIP service in the UK: all kinds of firms offer VoIP, including BT: its Broadband Voice service provides an adaptor that turns a normal phone into a VoIP one, and BT promises cheaper calls than with a traditional BT line. Other firms are clambering on the bandwagon too, and it's just a matter of time before every major telecommunications company offers a Voice over IP service. If you think you'll be making a lot of international calls, VoIP could save you a fortune.

Internet phone services such as Skype (**www.skype.com**) enable you to make free calls to other users and to save a fortune on international calls.

Getting on the broadband wagon

We've now mentioned broadband several times, so do you need it? The short answer is yes: super-fast, permanent internet connections make homeworking much more pleasant, and the fixed monthly charges mean that you don't need to watch the clock when you're online. Broadband also makes new technologies, such as Voice over IP phones, worthwhile. So what do you need and what should you watch out for?

There are two kinds of broadband: ADSL, which is delivered over the phone network, and cable, which uses the same network as cable TV. ADSL comes from BT and is sold by dozens of UK Internet Service Providers (ISPs) and cable is sold by cable firms such as NTL and Telewest. Both ADSL and cable offer very fast connections at decent prices, and the main difference between them is availability: if you can get cable TV you can probably get cable broadband; if you can't, you probably can't. Similarly if you've got a BT phone then you can probably get ADSL, although if you're in a rural area you might not be able to get the very fastest ADSL services. That's because ADSL needs you to be fairly close to the local phone exchange – within a couple of kilometres – in order to deliver its maximum speeds.

When you're choosing broadband there are three things to consider, or four if you include the price. You need to choose the speed of your connection, whether it's capped or uncapped, and whether you want the ISP to provide the hardware or choose it yourself.

You'll find that many ISPs offer two levels of service: home broadband and business broadband. The latter is always more

Broadband comes in two main flavours: ADSL, which is delivered via your BT phone line, and cable broadband, which uses cable networks from firms such as NTL.

expensive, but there's another key difference too. Broadband is contended, which means that multiple customers share the same equipment at the local exchange. With domestic broadband, the contention ratio is usually 50:1, which means the equipment is shared between 50 customers; with business broadband, the ratio is usually 20:1, which means you should get more consistent, faster performance than with a home broadband service. ISPs' terms and conditions generally state that you cannot use their home broadband services for business purposes, and ISPs reserve the right to cancel your broadband contract if you do.

Broadband speeds

Despite what some firms' ads would have you believe, connections slower than 512Kbps (kilobits per second) aren't broadband – although a 150Kbps service is certainly faster than a traditional modem connection, which runs out of steam at around 40Kbps. However, to get the full benefits of broadband, you'll need 512Kbps or more.

For a long time, 512Kbps was the fastest connection you could get, but as the technology has improved speeds have increased. Most firms offer affordable 1Mbps (1,000Kbps) and 2Mbps connections, while others are even faster: 8Mbps, 10Mbps and even 22Mbps in some cities. The cheapest services are usually the slowest, but even super-fast broadband isn't too expensive: at the time of writing, UK Online (**www.ukonline.co.uk**) offers 22Mbps broadband for £29.99 per month.

So do you need all that speed? Probably not. If you're just sending emails and browsing the internet, 512Kbps is perfectly adequate. However, if you need to download or upload big files, or if you plan to use services such as videoconferencing, then faster is better.

Firms such as UKOnline (**www.ukonline.co.uk**) offer super-speedy broadband services, but a basic broadband service is perfectly adequate for email, chat and browsing the internet.

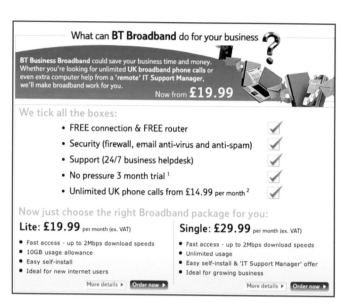

To cap or not to cap?

Many firms offer the same broadband product in two versions: capped and uncapped. Uncapped is always more expensive, because it means there's no limit to how much you download. If you spend all day every day downloading huge files, you won't pay any more than if you downloaded a single email every day.

Capped services, on the other hand, are limited. For example, Pipex's Start service (**www.solo.pipex.net**) gives you a 'usage allowance' of 1GB per month; if you want more you'll pay £2.70 for each 3GB block. One gigabyte of data sounds like a lot, but if you're downloading big files such as high-resolution digital photos, video clips, software programs or large, print-quality documents then you'll quickly reach the limit. It's worth shopping around: we've found that some ISPs offer uncapped services for the same price as their competitors' capped services.

Who supplies the hardware?

Many broadband ISPs have special offers where, if you sign up for broadband, they'll give you a free modem. That's not necessarily a bad deal, but there are limits to what your free modem can do. Such modems are typically basic USB models that aren't designed to do anything bar connect a single computer to the internet, so if you want to use your broadband connection for a network or wireless network you'd be better off supplying your own kit.

To use broadband over a network, you'll need a box called a router. This 'routes' network traffic, and it typically includes a connection for your phone line and then four or more ports for network connections. Wireless routers also have an antenna, which provides the signal for a wireless network.

Whether you go for a standard router or a wireless one, make sure it's the right kind of router: ADSL-compatible routers might not work with cable broadband, and vice versa. You might find that your ISP recommends a particular router and offers to sell one to you; if it does, do a quick search on a price comparison search engine such as Kelkoo (**www.kelkoo.com**) to see if you can get the same device for less money. In many cases, you'll find that you can.

You'll often find that the cheapest broadband services have a cap, or a 'usage limit'. This is how much data you can transfer per month, and if you exceed the limit you'll pay extra. For heavy use an unlimited broadband service is usually the better option.

You don't have to use the router suggested by your ISP: firms such as Netgear make a dizzying range of broadband routers, many of which enable you to share your connection via a wireless network.

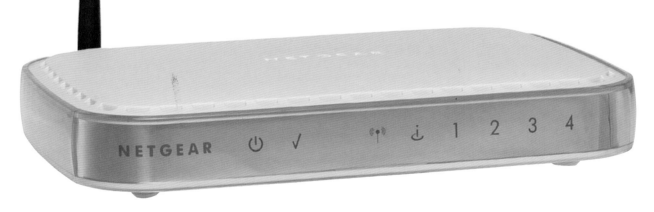

PART

Wired versus wireless

The simplest computer setup is a single machine with a broadband connection, but if you want to use more than one computer – or additional devices, such as a hybrid telephone that takes advantage of the internet or a network-aware printer that can be shared between several different computers – then you'll need a network. Networks come in two forms: wired and wireless.

Wired networks are by far the easiest to create: to share broadband between two PCs, all you need is a broadband router with a couple of Ethernet ports. Your computers need Ethernet ports too. Many computers – particularly laptops and desktops aimed at business users – have built-in Ethernet connections, but if your computer doesn't have one you can get an add-on card that slots inside your desktop PC's case or into your laptop's PC card slot.

Installing the network is simple. Connect your first PC via an Ethernet cable to the router and configure the router to access your broadband connection – all the information you need should be supplied by your ISP – and you're ready to go. Getting your second PC online is just a matter of getting a second Ethernet cable and plugging it into the router – and that's it.

It's a similar process with printers. If you choose a network-ready printer, it will have an Ethernet port; connect it to the router, install the print driver software (if necessary) on your computers, and then any machine on your network can print to the shared printer.

As you can see, it's very simple (and very cheap) but there are two big problems with wired networks. The first is that they need cables, which isn't ideal if you fancy accessing the internet from other rooms in the house or from the garden. The second is that Ethernet ports are quite big – the cable plugs are roughly the size of telephone plugs – so you can't easily fit them into small devices such as Pocket PCs or smartphones.

Wireless – known as Wi-Fi – networks solve both problems: because they use radio transmissions instead of cables you don't need to drill through walls if you want to use computers in other rooms, and in many cases you can browse the net from your shed if the signal's strong enough. We're writing this paragraph in

You can add wireless network support to almost any computer. Wireless adaptors come in PCI (for installing in desktop PCs), PC card (for laptops, as shown here) or USB flavours.

the garden: it's a sunny day and our wireless network means we're still receiving email while we're outside.

It's also relatively easy to put wireless network support into small devices, and you'll find that a growing number of Pocket PCs and even phones now support Wi-Fi technology. In the case of older Pocket PCs and other PDAs, you can buy tiny wireless network cards that simply plug into the device's storage card slot and turn it into a wireless machine.

Setting up a wireless network isn't much more difficult than setting up a wired one, and the equipment isn't much more expensive than wired networking equipment. However, wireless networking does raise some important issues that you might want to take into account.

Wireless standards

There are two main wireless standards: 802.11b and 802.11g. They both work in the same way but 802.11g is much faster than 802.11b and uses slightly different technology, so a wireless card that only supports the b standard won't be able to connect to a g network. However, most wireless cards now support both standards: look for products that are described as 802.11b/g and you'll be able to connect not just to your own wireless network, but to public wireless networks too.

There's a third standard, 802.11n. This is even faster than 802.11g, and it uses a technology called MIMO – multiple inputs, multiple outputs – to improve signal strength and speed. However, at the time of writing the 802.11n standard hasn't been finalised. That hasn't stopped companies selling 802.11n hardware, but beware: until the standard has been agreed by all the main players, you might find that so-called 'pre-n' hardware doesn't work properly with other firms' 802.11n products.

If that wasn't confusing enough, some manufacturers also offer their own versions of existing standards, so for example you'll see

Beware of 'standards' such as Super G: they're the manufacturer's own, so if you use other firms' equipment you might not get the advertised speeds.

wireless products advertised as 'Super G', which offer much faster speeds than 802.11g is supposed to deliver. Such products do work, but they only work with other products that use the same technology – so if you buy a Super G router but a standard 802.11g wireless network card, you won't get any benefit from the Super G technology.

Wireless speed and range

According to the blurb, 802.11b kit delivers connection speeds of 11Mbps while 802.11g kit increases it to 54Mbps. That's much faster than a broadband connection, but the figures are somewhat misleading. The figures you'll see on the box are maximums, and you'll never achieve them in the real world.

There are two reasons for this. The first is that the speed is shared by however many machines are connected, so if you have two computers accessing an 11Mbps connection then they get 5.5Mbps each. The speed also drops with distance – 802.11b's range is around 150 metres, but the signal strength drops dramatically long before that point, particularly if the signal has to pass through walls or other obstacles. The further you are from the wireless router, the slower your connection will be.

The second reason why the quoted speeds are over-optimistic is due to 'overheads'. Some of the data transferred between a wireless device and a wireless router is about the connection – essentially the router is asking 'is anybody there?' and your computer replies 'yes, I'm over here!' That chatter is essential to establish and maintain any wireless connection, but it takes a lot of data – typically 40 to 50% of the network connection. So your 11Mbps connection drops to around 5.5Mbps before you even get started, and when you connect a second PC the speed halves again to around 2.75Mbps – and it gets even slower the further away you are from the wireless router.

Does any of this matter? Yes and no. Even 2.75Mbps is fast enough for sharing a 512Kbps broadband connection, but there's not much point in spending money on a 22Mbps broadband connection if your wireless kit can't deliver it to your computer. That's why it makes sense to get the fastest wireless kit you can afford: the difference in price between 802.11b and 802.11g kit isn't dramatic, but if you're getting a fast broadband connection that you want to use with multiple computers then the faster kit is worth the extra expense.

Wireless security

The single best thing about wireless networks is that they work through walls. Unfortunately, the single worst thing about wireless networks is that they work through walls. As we write this – yes, we're still in the garden! – we're within range of two wireless networks: our own and our next-door neighbours'. They can't connect to our wireless network, but we can connect to theirs. That's because our wireless network is secure and theirs isn't.

It's very easy to secure a wireless network: when you buy a router, it has a range of security features built-in. For example, you can set a complicated password for your network, so anyone who doesn't know the password can't get on to your network; for extra security you can even create an 'access list' of computers. That turns your wireless router into an electronic bouncer: if a computer isn't on the list, it doesn't get into your network.

There are very good reasons for securing a wireless network, although they might not be obvious. For example, while the average person doesn't have the technical know-how to hack your system and steal your important files, if your network isn't secured it's child's play for anyone within range to connect and then use your internet connection. That's bad news for two reasons: they're getting free internet access that you're paying for and, more seriously, they could be up to no good. If they're caught, you could end up with the blame.

Choose a security type and enter the name of the AirPort network to join with an optional password.

Network Name: default

Wireless Security: WEP Password

Password:

☐ Show password

(?)   (Cancel) (OK)

The simplest way to secure your wireless network is to password-protect it. You'd be surprised how many people don't carry out this simple step.

Why letting other people use your internet connection is a bad idea

Whenever you connect to the internet, your ISP gives you a unique address, which is the internet equivalent of a telephone number. This address, known as the IP address, is logged – so if you try to hack into the Pentagon or look at illegal content, you can be traced. Although ISPs don't spy on you they do keep logs of IP addresses and their activity, and the police can compel them to hand over those logs if they believe a crime has been committed. When you use a wireless network, the IP address is assigned to your router and to any machine connected to it. That means that if someone else connects to your network, anything they do will still appear to come from your IP address.

Of course, you're a perfectly law-abiding, upstanding member of the public – but what about the people next door or people you haven't met? Although wireless networks don't extend too far, they do extend into the street – and as a lot of companies have discovered, that means people can sit outside in their cars and take advantage of wireless internet access for dodgy purposes. In the US, a number of people have been prosecuted for doing just that.

There's another, less dramatic reason not to share your broadband connection with other people: in most cases, your ISP's terms and conditions state that you can't share your broadband with anyone who doesn't share your building.

PART

Planning your office network

If you've decided that you'll need a network, it's worth spending a bit of time thinking about where everything's going to go. If you're going to use a wired network then it's a good idea to keep cable clutter to a minimum – partly because it's ugly, and partly because it can be a trip hazard. To minimise such clutter, it's a good idea to make the distance between the various items on your network – router, computers, printers – as short as possible. Remember too that the router needs to be connected to your broadband phone socket, so that needs to be included in your layout plans too.

With wireless networks you've got much more flexibility, because the only cable you'll need is the one connecting the wireless router to your broadband phone socket. It's still a good idea to think about office layout, though, because the location of your wireless router will make a big difference to the signal quality and therefore the speed of your wireless network. For best results, put your router somewhere away from too much metal (objects such as metal radiators or filing cabinets can cause problems) and, ideally, in a spot where there aren't any obstructions between the router and the devices you want to connect. If you fancy working from the garden, you'll get better results if you put the router on a windowsill that looks out on the garden than if the router's tucked away inside your house – but remember that it still needs to be connected to your broadband phone socket, so you'll need to decide on the best location for that too.

If you like the sound of working outside, consider a wireless rather than a wired network. It's easy to set up and means you can work from wherever you want.

PART **2**

How to buy your computing kit

You know what you need, but where should you buy your business bits and bobs? While it's possible to nip down to your local computing emporium and stock up on computers, printers and other essential equipment, it's not always the best – or the cheapest – way to do it.

Where to buy a computer

You can buy computers in any high street, but the stock is usually limited – and in many cases, you can find the same machines on the internet for considerably less cash. Some firms, such as PC giant Dell, don't sell their machines through the shops at all; instead, they sell machines over the phone or via their website (**www.dell.com/uk**). Because they don't have expensive high street premises to maintain, they can often sell computers for much less than you'd pay in the shops.

You can certainly save money by buying online, but shops have their benefits too. One of the main ones is that if you have a problem, you don't need to send your computer back to Ireland (or Amsterdam, or wherever the manufacturer is based) for repair; if you buy from an independent retailer, you might get better after-sales service or support than from a giant corporation. However, when you compare high-street prices with internet prices using a price comparison service such as Kelkoo (**www.kelkoo.com**), you'll also see that you pay a hefty premium for the personal touch.

Shopping search engines such as **Kelkoo.com** can save you a fortune by letting you see the best – and worst – prices from online retailers.

Price isn't the only reason why you might want to deal directly with the manufacturer. High-street shops don't provide the range of options you'll find online, because they're in the business of selling the machines on their shelves: if you want a particular machine but with a different optical drive, more memory and a faster hard disk, if the shop doesn't stock that particular configuration then you won't be able to buy it. The same applies to online computer shops that don't make the machines they sell: if they've got it, you can buy it. If they haven't, you can't.

If you know what you want, manufacturers' sites can be a better bet. Firms who build their machines to order enable you to customise every single component, so you can get a machine that meets your needs perfectly. The alternative – buying a PC off the shelf and then upgrading it later – is usually much more expensive. Build to order means you can't order a PC and have it that afternoon, but the savings mean it's usually worth waiting a week or two.

Many PCs are sold as bundles: buy this machine and get a free printer, or built-in wireless networking, or some other bit of equipment. However, some deals are better than others. Bundled printers or digital cameras tend to be fairly unsophisticated models, whereas integrated wireless networking or 'double memory for free!' deals are often worth taking advantage of. Don't let bundles blind you to the machine itself, though: if the machine isn't right for you, the inclusion of a printer you don't want and some software you'll never use won't make it any better.

How to pay for a computer

When you buy a computer there are usually several ways to pay for it. You can pay up-front, take a finance deal or, if you're a limited company, you can lease the equipment. Paying up-front is cheapest, but always use a credit card: that way if the company goes out of business before your machine arrives, or before the warranty expires, then you can file a claim with your credit card company to get your money back or to get the warranty honoured. That's because, when you pay with a credit card (not with a debit card or a credit card cheque), two contracts are formed. Your contract is with the credit card company, not the retailer, so if the retailer doesn't fulfil its side of the deal then the credit card company is liable.

It's important to note that credit cards won't protect you from some kinds of fraud: if you hand over your card details to a criminal, you're unlikely to get your money back. That's why if you shop online it's essential to use sites you trust. If you have the slightest doubt about a site, go elsewhere.

If you do pay by credit card, resist the temptation to leave the balance on your card. If you borrow £1,000 on a card and only make the minimum payment each month, depending on the card's interest rate it could take between 14 and 28 years to pay for your PC.

With finance deals you can spread the cost of a computer over 12, 24 or 36 months. Inevitably there's a cost for this, and it's important to check the small print carefully. Many finance deals charge very high interest rates, and it's often cheaper to get a personal loan from the bank or to use a credit card with a long 0% introductory offer.

For homeworkers, leasing is best avoided. As with finance deals, you pay a premium for the convenience of making monthly payments but, unlike with finance deals, you never own the equipment.

Many computer firms offer finance deals, which enable you to spread the cost over 1, 2 or 3 years. Compare the interest rate with a personal loan from your bank – the loan might be cheaper than the finance deal.

Where to buy printers, network cards and other equipment

When it comes to computer add-ons such as printers, wireless networking gear or other equipment, the best place to buy is usually online: a Netgear router from a shop is identical to one from an online retailer, and the difference in price can be dramatic. Savings of 30% compared to high street prices aren't unusual, and if you use a site such as Kelkoo to check prices you can find the best deals with hardly any effort. However, make sure you're comparing like with like: some sites charge what seem to be very cheap prices, but then expect you to pay hefty postage fees; others don't include VAT. Whether you're using a price-checking service or browsing from shop to shop, make sure you're comparing the price you'll actually pay rather than the headline price.

As with computers, when you buy add-ons or consumables online you should always follow the golden rules: don't buy from sites you don't trust 100% and always pay with your credit card.

Buying equipment on eBay

Online auction sites such as eBay (**www.ebay.co.uk**) and QXL (**www.qxl.com**) can be a great source of bargains, but there are risks: when the hammer falls, you can't change your mind. Because you can't pop round to the seller's house and see a laptop before pledging your cash, it's essential that you know exactly what you're bidding for.

With online auctions you need to read the item descriptions carefully and, if anything is unclear, ask lots of questions. Use the seller's feedback rating to get an idea of his or her trustworthiness; if the seller is new to the site and has no feedback from previous auctions, it doesn't mean they're dodgy, but it does mean you should be very careful and ask lots of questions about the machine, its history, whether the seller has the original software discs and so on.

Make sure the machine is actually in the UK and is a UK-specification machine, too: imports are worth less money, and if your computer is being shipped from the US there's an increased risk of damage in transit. You're also liable for VAT and other duty on any purchase from outside the EU; for a £1,000 laptop that could add several hundred pounds to the price tag. There have also been a number of cases of auction fraud involving sellers from Eastern Europe who ask for cash payments or bank credit transfers: another good reason to stick with UK sellers.

The risk of fraud is minimal – eBay claims that fewer than 0.01% of auction sales are fraudulent – but it's still a risk: while every eBay transaction is covered by the site's Buyer Protection Programme, it will only pay compensation of up to £120. If you have the slightest doubt about the seller or the item they're selling then don't place a bid.

Beware of commercial traders pretending to be normal users: the average person doesn't have the capability to accept credit card payments, so if a supposedly private seller can take Mastercard or Visa (without using an intermediary such as PayPal or NoChex) then they're probably a commercial operation. There are plenty of traders on auction sites who are honest, but the ones who pretend to be private sellers are trying to evade the Distance Selling Regulations and the Sale of Goods Act.

We'd strongly recommend the use of an escrow service, too. With normal auctions the process is simple: you pay the seller, and the seller ships the goods. However with big ticket items such as laptops that's a fairly risky procedure, and it's possible that the seller could take your cash and do a disappearing act. To prevent this, an escrow service will charge you a small fee to act as a middleman. You lodge your payment with the escrow service, and the seller doesn't get the cash until the goods have been delivered. If you're planning to spend several hundred pounds on a computer and the seller isn't willing to use the escrow service – even if you pay the escrow fee – then it should once again set alarm bells ringing.

Finally, beware of auction fever. Many people end up paying over the odds because they think that if it's an auction sale, it must be a bargain; in some cases, items sell for more money than brand new models cost in the shops. Do your homework, research prices and identify the going rate for your chosen hardware, then set a budget and stick to it.

This auction for a Sony laptop might be perfectly honest, but we wouldn't bid: the seller is outside the UK, and doesn't publish comments from previous buyers.

Sites such as **Loot.com** can be a tremendous source of second-hand computing kit if you take the same precautions you would with any other private sales.

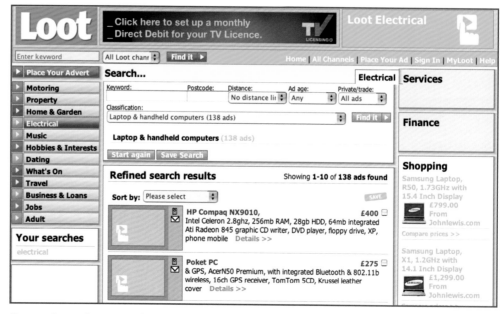

Scouring the small ads

As with auctions, most small-ad sellers are perfectly reputable; however, when you consider that 67,000 laptops were stolen in the UK in 2004 alone, it's sensible to be suspicious. Not all stolen machines are sold in pubs or from the backs of lorries.

It's important to tread carefully with second-hand equipment because if you buy a machine privately and something goes wrong, you're not protected by consumer legislation. The Sale of Goods Act does apply to private sales, but only in a limited way: the goods must be safe and 'as described'; if not, you have the right to seek a refund. In practice, getting a refund from a private seller may require a trip to the courts.

So what should you look for? Beware of dodgy dealers, people in the PC sales business who pretend to be private advertisers. In many cases they do this to avoid paying tax, but in some cases they are doing it so you don't have any comeback should your purchase pack up. Tell-tale signs are adverts offering new, boxed machines – would *you* buy a brand new laptop and sell it without even taking it out of the packaging? – or adverts offering multiple machines; see if the same phone number appears on different ads, and look for any mention of VAT. Private customers neither know nor care about VAT, but traders do. Remember that it's illegal for traders to pose as private sellers, so if they're willing to break that law you can't expect them to be honest about anything else.

It's essential that you see the computer for yourself before buying, either in the seller's home or workplace. Any other meeting place should set alarm bells ringing. When you get there check the screen for dead pixels, make sure that any connectors aren't bent and look for obvious signs of damage that might indicate the machine hasn't been well looked after. Check that any supplied peripherals (keyboards, mice, add-on cards) actually work, and in the case of laptops make sure the machine functions when it's unplugged from the mains – and that the battery charges when you plug it back in again.

Ask if the seller has the original receipt – many legitimate sellers will have – and make sure there are discs to match the supplied software. When you buy a computer it's a very good idea to reformat the hard disc and reinstall the software and any necessary

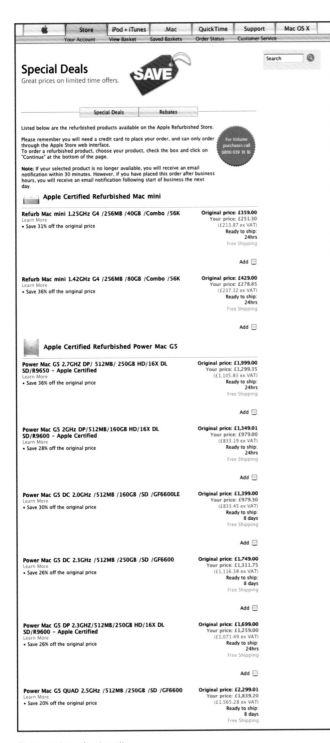

Firms such as Apple sell refurbished machines at huge discounts, but don't expect the very latest models.

drivers; if you don't have the discs, you may have to buy Windows, Office and any other key programs. Be particularly wary of any seller offering big-name products such as Photoshop, Office or other goodies if they don't have the CDs: it's a good indication that the software is illegal. Most importantly, ask questions. If you feel the seller isn't telling the whole truth, take your money elsewhere.

The best of both worlds?

If you'd like the savings of second-hand equipment but don't fancy the risks, there are two other options: end-of-line stock and refurbished machines. You'll find end-of-line stock offered by firms such as Morgan Computers (**www.morgancomputers.com**), while Dell and Apple – not to mention independents such as Cancom UK – sell refurbished machines.

If a computer is described as end-of-line stock, it means that that particular model has been discontinued – usually to make way for a newer, sleeker model. While some end-of-line stock is positively ancient, there are plenty of decent machines out there with very low price tags. If you don't need the very latest model, you can get a very powerful machine for surprisingly little money.

Refurbished machines – 'refurbs' for short – are slightly different. When Apple or Dell sells a machine, if it's returned with a minor fault, they can't simply fix the problem and sell it as new. Instead, they shift the stock through firms such as Cancom UK (**www.cancomuk.com**) or through their own outlets – the Apple Refurbished Store (**http://promo.euro.apple.com/promo/refurb/uk/**) and Dell Outlet (**www1.euro.dell.com/content/default.aspx?c= uk&l=en&s=dfo**). In addition to repaired machines, both outlets also sell returned stock from cancelled orders and, occasionally, ex-lease equipment. The available discounts vary, but it's not unusual to see refurb machines being sold with 45% off the list price.

When you're considering refurb kit, it's important to know the potential downsides. Refurbs are rarely the most up-to-date models, so if you're expecting 45% off the very latest Apple MacBook you'll probably be disappointed. Make sure you know exactly what you're getting, too: for example, the desktops Dell sells in its Outlet don't come with monitors. In most cases you won't be able to finance your purchase, either: both Dell and Apple expect you to pay in full when you order.

Other things to consider are the machine's appearance – it's likely to have a few scratches or discolouration – and warranty support. If you buy from Cancom you get a three-month warranty (unless the product is marked as an Apple Refurb, in which case you get a 12-month warranty); buy direct from Dell or Apple and you get a standard one-year limited warranty. However, in most cases if your refurbished machine has a fault on arrival, you can't get it repaired or replaced; instead, the manufacturer will arrange for the machine to be returned and your money to be refunded.

Are warranties worth it?

When you work from home, your computer isn't something you can manage without: if it isn't working, neither are you. The more computerised your job, the more disastrous a computer

Cover It with Dell Support Services

3-Year International On-site service ▲

 Dell Service Solutions. Created with you in Mind.
Flexible service offerings from Dell

❓ Learn More

○ 1-Year On-site service [subtract £176.25]

◉ 3-Year International On-site service [Included in Price]
Dell Recommended

○ 4-Year International On-site service [add £47.00 or £1/month[1]]

Many computer firms offer a range of extended warranties with their products. It's a very good idea to check the details of cover carefully to be sure you're getting value for money.

problem would be. So should you spend extra money on a warranty? For most people the answer is 'probably not', but in the case of homeworkers it's a bit more complicated than that.

If you don't pay for an extended warranty or support package, you're still covered in the event of disaster. Most manufacturers offer a one-year warranty, and you're also covered under the Sale of Goods Act. However, standard warranties are usually return-to-base, which means the manufacturer will collect your machine and send it away for repair – and it won't provide you with a replacement to tide you over. Many firms put a strict time limit on such repairs – for example, Dell promises to fix a faulty business PC within six days – but others don't, and repairs can take a while. When our laptop recently developed a minor fault, we had to manage without it for six weeks.

Computer firms will typically offer two kinds of extra cover: longer warranty periods, or enhanced services. You could replace the one-year warranty with a three-year warranty, or perhaps boost the level of cover from return-to-base to on-site service. Naturally this costs money. For example, to increase the cover on an Apple MacBook Pro from one year to three years, you'll pay an extra £279; if you want to upgrade the cover on a £279 Dell desktop to include accidental damage, you'll pay an extra £70.50. That sounds reasonable, but it's a quarter of the price of the computer – and your home insurance policy may already include accidental damage cover for all your electronic equipment, not just your PC.

Different firms offer different warranties, so if you're finding it hard to choose between otherwise identical (and identically priced) machines, go for the one with the better warranty package. However, if you're considering paying extra for an extended warranty check what it covers very carefully. You might find that it's cheaper to stick with the standard warranty cover and buy a second, bargain basement computer that you can fall back on if disaster strikes.

By now you should have everything you need to choose your computer hardware and the add-ons you need too. The next step is to get the software to make the most of it – and that's what we'll explore in Part 3.

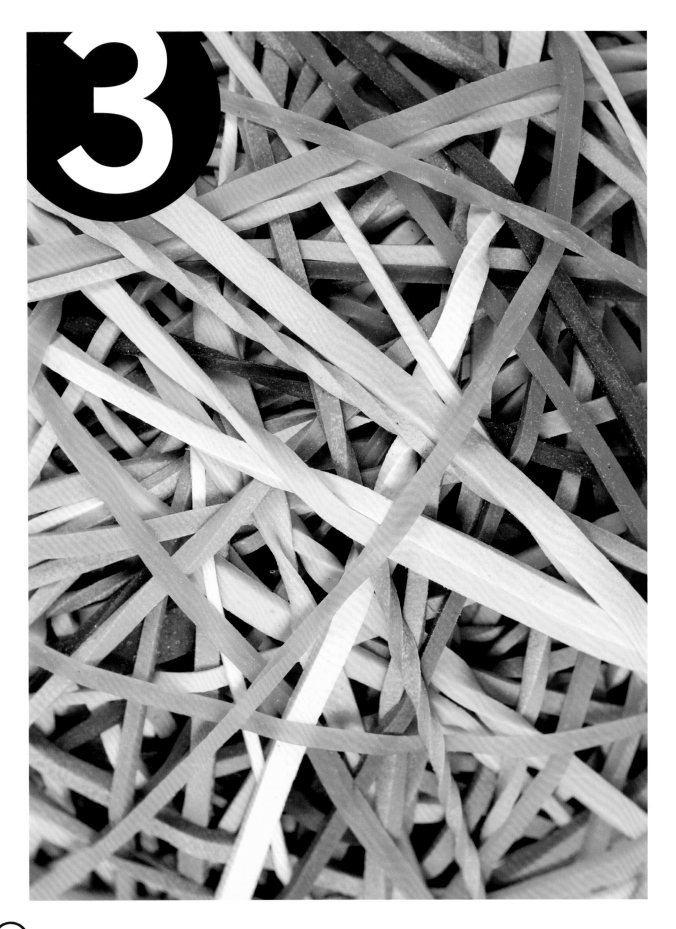

3

WORKING FROM HOME MANUAL

Smart software

Whether you're running a PC or a Mac, there's a huge range of software to choose from. In addition to specialist software for particular jobs – photo and video editing, design software and so on – there are programs that can make any homeworker's life easier. From automating your office to managing messages, digitising documents to tracking your tax bill, the right programs can make you more efficient. If time is money, then the right software can save you a fortune.

You can save money in other ways, too. While the best-known programs are often expensive, you'll often find bargain basement alternatives that cover the essentials just as well – and sometimes, even better. Thanks to the Open-source movement there's an ever-growing amount of free software too, and some of it is exceptionally good – so good, in fact, that some governments are ditching famous-name programs and embracing open-source software instead.

In this part, we'll discover the best tools to help you get things done – no matter how big or how small your budget may be.

SMART SOFTWARE
Office essentials

Office suites are particularly handy for homeworkers, as they cover the everyday essentials of business life: writing documents, creating invoices, preparing presentations, keeping track of budgets and so on. When you buy a new computer you might get a suite as part of the package: Microsoft Office or Microsoft Works on a PC, or the iWork suite on the Mac. They aren't the only options, though. As we'll discover, you can get excellent office software without spending a fortune and, in some cases, you can get it for free.

There are lots of office programs on the market, but these are the key ones to consider.

Microsoft Office

http://office.microsoft.com
Around £300
PC or Mac

The best-known office suite on the planet is now in its twelfth edition but, while there's no doubt that it's a heavyweight package, it's also rather expensive. There are several versions available but the two key editions are Standard, which gives you Word, Excel, Outlook and Powerpoint for around £300, and Professional, which costs about £50 more and adds Publisher and Access to the package (although as we went to press Microsoft was preparing a brand new version of Office, so prices may change).

So what do these programs actually do?
● Outlook is a communications package that combines email with calendars and to-do lists. You can use it to plan projects or remind you of important tasks, and as it's designed for business users it comes with lots of powerful features. For example, you can get Outlook to check incoming messages, get rid of the junk mail, highlight important emails and even automatically file messages away. Outlook has also been designed to synchronise with Pocket PCs and Windows-powered smartphones, so you can take your messages, to-do lists and appointments with you.
● Word is a word processor that's designed for everything from dashing off the odd letter to writing an entire book (this manual was written in Word). It's very powerful and includes key features such as mail merge, which enables you to send personalised letters to a database of people without having to create a new document for each contact, automatic spelling and grammar checking, and reviewing. Reviewing is particularly useful if you collaborate on documents with others: you can send your colleagues a Word document, they

can make changes or comments, and when the document comes back you can see their amendments and decide whether or not to accept them.

- Excel is a spreadsheet for number crunching, although it's also good at managing simple lists for jobs such as mail merges. We use it to keep track of tax and other important financial things, and the program also makes it easy to analyse and present data. In particular Excel has an excellent chart engine that can turn dull rows of figures into eye-catching 3D graphs.

- PowerPoint is the presentation program, and if you've seen slides on a big screen recently it's almost certainly been powered by PowerPoint. The program provides you with a range of templates, and you can build a presentation in a matter of minutes before taking it on the road and wowing potential clients.

If you go for the Professional edition you also get Publisher, a page layout program that's good for putting together brochures, and Access, a very powerful database system. However it's worth noting that Word's page layout features are good too, and Excel's well suited to managing everyday lists such as a simple list of clients.

There's also a version of Office for the Mac, but it's quite different from the PC version. Outlook is replaced by Entourage, which does much the same thing as Outlook but looks very different, and while you get Word, Excel and PowerPoint there are slight differences between the PC and Mac versions. The most obvious difference is in the way they look: the Mac versions have slightly different user interfaces to make them more Mac-like.

Publisher and Access are not available on the Mac, so the Mac version of Office Professional comes with the Virtual PC program, which you can use to run PC software (slowly!) on your Mac. At the time of writing Virtual PC only runs on older Macs such as the Powerbook G4 or the iMac G5: if you've got an Intel-powered Mac such as the latest iMac or the MacBook Pro, Virtual PC won't work.

Whether you go for the PC or Mac version of Office, you definitely get a lot for your money – but that strength is also one of Office's weaknesses. Research suggests that most people only use 20% of what Office can actually do, so while Word includes some powerful features for creating books and other complex documents, many people only use it for creating letters and the odd memo. Similarly Excel is quite at home carrying out impossibly complex and arcane financial modelling, but many people use it to keep track of their expenses.

If you need the package's power then we think Office is worth the money, but if you don't plan to take advantage of the advanced features then it's a bit like buying a Ferrari and never taking it out of first gear. Before spending a few hundred pounds on Office, it's worth considering some more modest – and more affordable – alternatives.

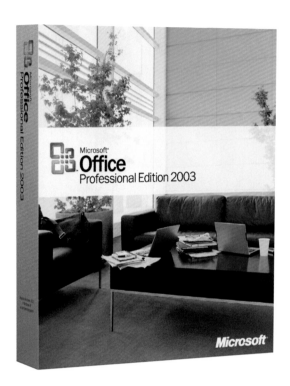

Microsoft Works

www.microsoft.com/products/works

£30 to £70

PC only

Microsoft Works is Office for people who don't need Office, and it's aimed squarely at home users and small businesses. It comes in two versions: Works 8, which costs around £30, and Works Suite 2006, which costs around £70. Both versions include word processing, spreadsheet, calendar and project organising tools, but the Suite adds some extra programs: the basic word processor is replaced with a full copy of Microsoft Word and you also get Digital Image Standard for photo editing, the Encarta encyclopaedia for reference, Microsoft Money for keeping track of your income and expenditure, and the route planning program Autoroute Essentials.

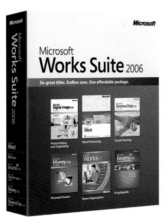

You can't argue with a price tag that's one-tenth of the cost of Microsoft Office but, as you'd expect, Works and Works Suite are much more limited than Microsoft Office – and the bundled programs are generally good for home users, but less useful for business users. For example Microsoft Money is an excellent program for managing your personal finances, but it's not designed to deal with business finances – so if you need a package that creates and helps you keep track of invoices, Money isn't for you. The word processor (in Works 8) and spreadsheet (in both versions) are very basic, and Works can view but not create PowerPoint presentations. Finally Autoroute Essentials is a decent mapping program that provides good driving directions, but you can get much the same thing online for free via Google Maps (**http://maps.google.com**).

Both versions of Works are fine products, but they're best suited to home use and very basic business tasks: we suspect the typical customer uses Works to manage the family finances and send the odd letter, tasks for which it's ideal. If you need something a bit more ambitious, we think you'll find Works too limited.

Ability Office

www.ability.com

Around £50

PC only

Like Microsoft Office, Ability Office comes in several different versions – but unlike Microsoft Office, the most expensive version is still only £50. If you can live without a presentation program and a database application you can get the suite for just £29.99.

If you go for the most expensive edition, Ability Office Professional, you get six programs: Write, the word processor; Spreadsheet, for number crunching; Presentation, for PowerPoint-style presenting; Database, for managing complex information; Photopaint, for image creation and editing; and Photoalbum, for organising your digital images.

The most striking thing about Ability Office is the way it looks, particularly when you use the word processing or spreadsheet programs. They look almost identical to Microsoft Word and Microsoft Excel, so if you've used Office 97, 2000 or Office XP you'll feel right at home. The programs can also read and write Office documents, although there are a few compatibility issues: for example when you import an Excel spreadsheet into Ability Spreadsheet, it calculates dates in a different way from Excel –

which means that any dates in the imported spreadsheet will be inaccurate. It's a common problem with Office-compatible suites, and it's a reminder that while it's usually possible to read and write Office documents the process isn't always trouble-free.

Is Ability Office a genuine alternative to Microsoft Office? For everyday tasks, yes. However, it can struggle with more complex documents such as Word files with embedded charts, so it's worth downloading the trial version (which is free from **www.ability.com**) and putting it through its paces to make sure it can cope with the jobs you need it to do.

iWork '06

www.apple.com/iwork

Mac only

£69

Apple's iWork suite takes a very different approach to office software. Instead of four, five or six different programs, you get two: Pages, for creating documents, and Keynote, for delivering presentations. Both programs come with some exceptionally good-looking templates that make it easy to create smart-looking documents or presentations in seconds, and Keynote is particularly good: thanks to the graphics technology inside every Mac, it produces high-quality presentations that look good enough to eat and which PowerPoint users can only dream of.

Pages is less successful. Although you can use it for word processing and even mail merges, it's best suited to page-layout work – so if you want to create brochures, flyers or other marketing materials, Pages will be right up your street. It's less impressive for everyday word processing, though, and we've found that it struggles to keep up with our typing.

iWork is typically Apple: it looks good and takes a completely different approach to every other software firm. When it's good, it's very good, and if your main requirement is a good presentation program then Keynote will knock your socks off.

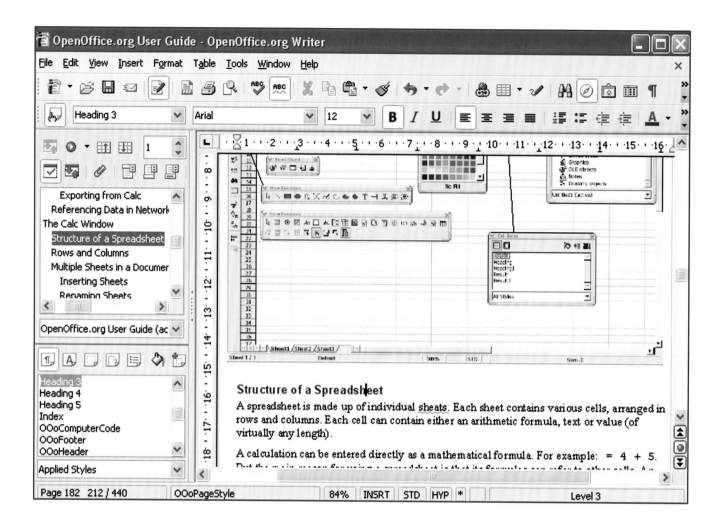

OpenOffice.org 2.0

www.openoffice.org

PC, Mac or Linux

Free

OpenOffice.org is a very credible rival to Microsoft Office. It can read and write Office documents and it can do most of the things the various parts of Microsoft Office can do – but it's completely free. It's also available for a range of operating systems including Windows, Mac OS X and Linux, so no matter what kind of computer you have you'll be able to find a version of OpenOffice.org to run on it. There's even a portable version that you can download and put on a USB pen drive, which means you can take the entire suite wherever you go and run it on any computer you like.

So what do you get for no money? There are six programs in the OpenOffice.org suite: Writer, for word processing; Impress, for presentations; Math, for mathematical calculations; Draw, for creating and editing images; Calc, for spreadsheet work; and Base, for managing databases.

As with Ability Office, OpenOffice.org looks very like Office XP, so you don't need to worry about learning a whole new way of doing things. There are a few differences – things you'd expect to find under one menu appearing under another one – but there's

nothing too dramatic, and OpenOffice.org is a nice place to spend time in. It's also very powerful and, like Microsoft Office, it's ideal for beginners and advanced users alike. However, as with most Office-a-likes don't be surprised if you encounter the odd problem when you try to import files created in Word and Excel. If presentation software is a key requirement then you might find the Impress program less impressive than rival products.

For most jobs, OpenOffice.org is very impressive, but there is one key issue that you might want to consider. When you use most software, there's a technical support department you can call; with OpenOffice.org, there isn't. You can find answers to most questions on the internet, but if you want the reassurance of knowing that you can telephone an expert when things go wrong, then OpenOffice isn't for you.

So how can OpenOffice.org give you a fully featured office suite for free? The reason is a philosophy called Open Source, which is responsible for producing lots of high-quality software and then giving it away for nothing.

SMART SOFTWARE

Free as a bird

Open Source is all about free software. However, while most of the best-known programs are indeed free, the movement's philosophy is free as in 'free speech' rather than 'free beer': there's nothing to stop firms making their own versions of open-source programs and charging money for them, or offering programs on CD and then charging for the disc.

The open-source movement is a reaction to traditional software firms, who release products but prohibit you from fiddling with them – so if you're a programmer who thinks Microsoft Word would be better if you did some tweaking, tough luck. The open source philosophy is best described as 'the more the merrier': the more people contributing their expertise to a program, the better the program will be. There are no secrets in open source, either. If you contribute to an open-source program you agree that others can look at what you've done and make changes to it. The result of all of this is a huge army of software developers producing some interesting products. In many cases, open-source programs are better than anything from big name firms such as Microsoft or Apple.

Enough of the theory. What does this mean for you? Thanks to open source, you can get everything from your computer's operating system to a web browser, email program and even an entire office suite for free. You won't get technical support – in most cases, if something goes wrong you're on your own – but when you see what you can get for nothing, we think you'll be impressed.

We've already discovered OpenOffice.org, the open source alternative to Microsoft Office, but there are lots of other powerful programs to choose from. These are the most common alternatives to other big-name programs.

Linux instead of Windows

Linux is an alternative operating system. It runs on most PCs and some firms also make versions of Linux for Macs. It looks and works very like Windows or OS X, but unlike those operating systems it won't cost you a penny unless you buy it on CD – and even then, you'll only pay a few pounds. There are lots of free versions of Linux available for download. For example, you can download a full version of Fedora, one of the many flavours of Linux, for free from **http://fedora.redhat.com**.

Linux is very fast and very secure, and it can give a new lease of life to older computers that struggle to run the latest versions of Windows or Mac OS X. However, there are some problems too. You can't run non-Linux software very easily (it's possible via emulation software, but you're better off with programs designed specifically for Linux – there are lots to choose from) and there's no technical support unless you pay a firm to provide it. It's not quite as beginner-friendly as Windows or OS X, and you'll probably encounter the odd hardware problem. For example, we installed Linux on one of our PCs and it ran like a dream, but it

Ubuntu (**www.ubuntu.com**) is one of many versions of the free Linux operating system, which is a direct rival to Windows and Mac OS X.

didn't recognise our wireless network adapter – and while there's a tweak that would make it work, it was far too complicated for us to attempt.

If you're the kind of person who'd rather not fiddle around with your computer then Linux isn't for you, but if you enjoy the technical side of things then Linux is a very powerful and very useful operating system.

Firefox instead of Internet Explorer

The Firefox web browser is available for Linux, Windows and Mac OS X, and you can download it from **www.mozilla.com/firefox**. It offers several advantages over browsers such as Internet Explorer or Apple's Safari. It's a very solid and secure browser that doesn't suffer from the virus and malicious software that target Internet Explorer in particular and, unlike Internet Explorer and Safari, it's almost infinitely customisable. If you don't like the way Firefox looks you

Firefox is a superb web browser and you can make it even better by downloading free 'extensions' to add new features or block content you don't want to see.

can completely transform its appearance by downloading a free theme.

You can change Firefox in other ways, too. Programmers have created a huge range of extensions, programs designed to plug in to Firefox and add new features. Like Firefox, the extensions are free and you can find extensions for almost any purpose. There are extensions that make it easy to update a weblog from within Firefox; extensions that block animated adverts; extensions that download entire sites so you can look at them later; and you can even download extensions that do complicated things such as transforming the way famous sites look, or blocking messages on discussion forums from people that don't interest you.

At the time of writing Microsoft is preparing a brand new version of Internet Explorer that's designed to catch up with Firefox, but we've used it and we think Firefox is still the better browser. If you haven't already tried it, we'd strongly recommend giving it a go.

Thunderbird instead of Outlook or Outlook Express

Thunderbird is the email equivalent of Firefox and if you're currently using Microsoft's Outlook Express then you should switch: Thunderbird is much more powerful and, more importantly, much more secure than Microsoft's basic email program. It's also a credible rival to Outlook: while it doesn't have calendar features or scheduling options, it's much better at managing email and it's particularly good at filtering out junk mail. One of its best features is its support for multiple email accounts: you can use one copy of Thunderbird for several email accounts, so for example you can use it to access your personal email and business email while keeping the various messages separate from one another.

You can download Thunderbird for free from **www.mozilla.com/thunderbird**.

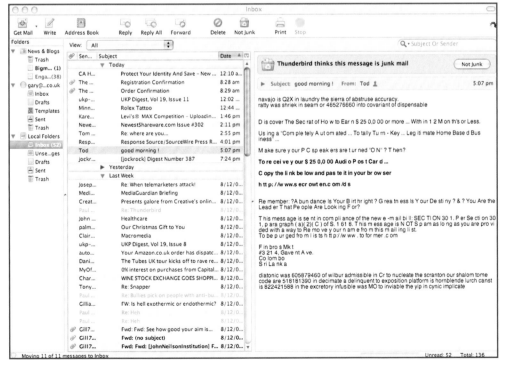

Thunderbird is the email equivalent of Firefox. It includes a very effective junk email filter that can dramatically reduce the amount of dodgy mail you receive.

GIMP isn't quite as user-friendly as more mainstream image editors, but it's an excellent graphics program that doesn't cost a penny.

GIMP instead of Photoshop

Adobe's Photoshop is the leading program for creating and editing graphics, but GIMP is a good alternative. It's nowhere near as user-friendly as Photoshop – it's not really suitable for complete beginners – but, if you're willing to spend some time getting to grips with it, you'll find that GIMP is very powerful and can create some very nifty visual effects.

Once again, GIMP is free and you'll find the Windows, Mac and Linux versions at **www.gimp.org**.

Nvu instead of FrontPage

Web-design software is becoming more and more common in home offices, especially for self-employed people who use their websites as online brochures. One of the best-known web-design programs is Microsoft's FrontPage, but there's an open source equivalent: Nvu is available for free from **www.nvu.com** and is available for Windows, Mac OS X and Linux.

Nvu is very easy to use and it includes all the tools you need for creating and editing web pages and uploading the finished masterpieces to your site. In fact, we used Nvu for our Web Design Manual!

Nvu looks simple, but it's a deceptively powerful web-editing program that you can use to create, edit and publish entire websites.

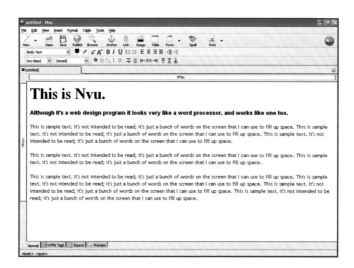

SMART SOFTWARE

Do you need software at all?

The programs we've looked at so far all have one thing in common: to use them, you need to install them on your desktop or laptop computer. However, a new breed of programs works in a very different way: instead of installing them you simply access them through your web browser. You can use word-processing software, spreadsheet software, email software, calendar software, ... if you can imagine it, there's probably a website that offers it. Even better, most such sites are free. So should you forget about buying or downloading stand-alone applications and embrace online software instead?

There are several key benefits to web-based software. In most cases, traditional software costs a great deal of money, but most online applications are free. They're also platform-independent, which means that you can use them on a Windows PC, a Mac or a Linux computer; in some cases you can even use them from a smartphone or a Pocket PC. They're also updated immediately, so if they need a security fix or a bug fix you don't need to download it. Instead, the next time you access the program you'll automatically use an updated version. Finally, many online programs enable you to store documents online, which means you can work from anywhere you can get internet access instead of having to carry your documents around with you on a USB flash drive or a CD.

If that sounds too good to be true, you may be right. For all the benefits of using web-based programs, there are plenty of negatives too:

● **It's only as fast as your internet connection**
Online applications depend on computers that may be hundreds or even thousands of miles away, and if the connections between you and those computers are congested then the performance of the program will deteriorate dramatically.

● **No connection, no software**
As you'd expect, you can't access online software if you can't get online – so for example you won't be able to use it if you're on a plane or if you can't get internet access in some way. When you're on the move, it's possible to get online with a laptop and a mobile phone but such connections are very slow, very expensive and, in our experience, very unreliable.

● **It might not always be available**
We're big fans of online email systems such as Google Mail (**http://mail.google.com**), but we regularly encounter periods when the service isn't available – which means our email isn't

available either. Other online services suffer from the same problems so, for example, you might find that when you try to access the service to do something important it's 'temporarily unavailable' due to 'scheduled maintenance'.

● **It might not be very good**

Some online services (such as, Google Mail and the 30boxes calendar system at **http://30boxes.com**) are very good. However, many online services aren't. For example, ajaxWrite (**www.ajaxwrite.com**) was launched amid claims that 'for 90% of the people in the world, the need to buy Microsoft Word just vanished' but, in our experience, it's very basic, very slow and prone to crashing. It's a similar story with the online graphics program ajaxSketch (**www.ajaxsketch.com**), which has been described as an alternative to high-end graphics programs such as Adobe Illustrator. It's nothing of the sort.

● **There's no technical support**

With traditional software, there's usually a helpline you can call if you encounter trouble. With web-based software, there isn't.

● **If the site disappears, so does the software**

Google isn't likely to disappear any time soon, but what about the other online services? There are lots of similar applications, so in the world of online word processors and spreadsheets there are dozens of sites offering essentially the same kinds of software. Inevitably some of those sites won't last and, if you choose one of the ones that doesn't last the course, then there's always the risk that it'll disappear overnight and take the software – and your documents – with it.

● **It might not be free forever**

Most online applications are free, especially the ones labelled 'beta' (more of that in a moment). However, there's no way to predict whether a particular program will stay free forever, or whether it'll cost money at a later date. If you come to depend on a particular program and the developers decide to charge for it, you'll either have to pay up or spend lots of time moving your data to an alternative program.

● **It's usually in beta**

If – like most online applications we've seen – a program is labelled as a 'beta' or a 'preview', that means it isn't finished. Beta is computer-industry shorthand for 'help us find the bugs' and it's generally accepted that beta software might do strange things, crash your computer or even destroy your data. That's fine if you want to experiment with cutting-edge technology, but if you use beta software (whether it's online or on your computer) for business-critical tasks then you're taking a very big risk.

Web-based services are improving quickly and in a few years, they could well be a better option than traditional programs. However, for now we think the negatives vastly outweigh the benefits and we'd stick with traditional software, whether that's a big-name package such as Microsoft Office or an open source alternative such as OpenOffice.org.

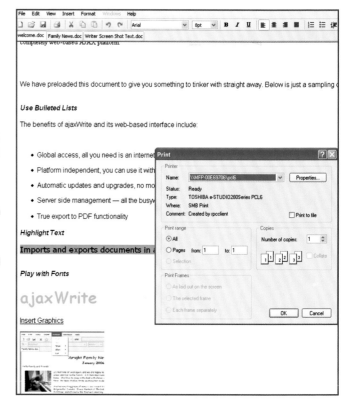

Web-based programs such as ajaxWrite promise to do everything Microsoft Word does, but we've found most such programs to be very basic and, in some cases, desperately slow too.

SMART SOFTWARE

Paperless offices and digital documents

When computers first arrived, excitable pundits said that we'd soon have paperless offices. They were wrong: computers mean we're using more paper than ever before.

That doesn't mean you can't have a paperless office, though. Scanners and multi-function printers make it easy to turn paper documents into digital ones, which can prevent you from being buried under a mountain of paperwork. Digital filing is particularly useful if you're short of space but need to hang on to lots of documents for future reference: you can get thousands of pages on a single CD, or millions of pages on a hard disk.

A word of warning: if you're storing important documents digitally and you don't keep the originals, then a reliable backup system is even more important than before. Computers can and do break; computers can be stolen; and it's all too easy to delete important files by accident. It doesn't matter whether your backups are to an external hard disk, to CD or to storage space on the internet: if files on your computer are important, you need to make backup copies. Think of it as your electronic insurance against digital disasters.

To digitise documents you'll need two things: a scanner (or a multifunction printer that includes a scanner) and suitable software. Most scanners come with software that's designed to help you scan and store documents, but you can also buy software from third parties that does more interesting things. For example Abbyy Finereader Professional (from **www.abbyy.com**, around £89) not only scans documents, but converts them too – so you can scan a report and save it as an editable Word document, or scan pages of figures and store them as Excel files. The program can also convert digital PDF files into Word documents, which could prove handy: PDF files are usually very difficult to edit, but with FineReader you can save them in the format of your choice and make any changes you wish.

Programs such as Abbyy FineReader enable you to turn scanned documents into editable ones, or to edit PDF files created by others.

PART **3**

Ten tools for happier homeworking

No two homeworkers are alike and the software you'll use to get the job done will depend on the job you're doing – so while a writer will depend on word-processing software, a graphic designer needs a powerful graphics program and a web designer needs web-design software. However, no matter what kind of work you do, there are ten tools that can make every homeworker's life easier.

Anti-virus software

Accessing the internet without up-to-date anti-virus software is a very bad idea: an unprotected PC will be infected with malicious software within minutes of getting online, and if your computer gets infected you could suffer problems ranging from poor performance to damaged data. In some cases it's even possible for the creators of malicious software to spy on what you're doing, for example by capturing your credit card details.

Virus-scanning software such as McAfee's Viruscan can protect your PC from net nasties – provided you keep its virus database up to date.

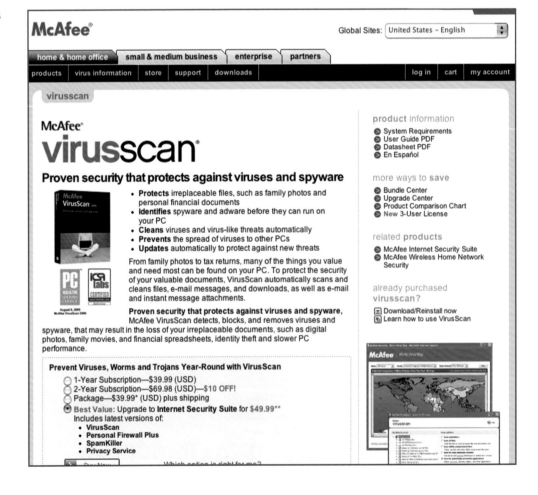

Anti-virus software needn't be expensive – you can get free PC anti-virus software from **www.grisoft.com**, while firms such as McAfee, Symantec and Zone Labs all offer reasonably priced anti-virus packages – but when you're choosing a program make sure that its list of viruses is updated at least daily, and that such updates are included in the price. With new viruses discovered daily, virus protection that doesn't get updated is useless – so when you've got the software, make sure you keep it up to date!

Junk mail filters

Time spent sorting through junk email, get-rich-quick schemes and frauds is time you can't spend on your job. A good anti-spam filter will get rid of the junk and leave legitimate messages alone, and the more emails you get the more important such filters become. Around 65% of our incoming messages are junk, and our anti-spam software gets rid of them so we can concentrate on more important things.

As with anti-virus software there's a huge range of programs to choose from. We particularly like SpamSieve for the Mac (around £12 from **http://c-command.com**); on the PC, the same firms who make anti-virus products also make very effective anti-spam filters too. If you're considering such products it might be worth buying an entire security suite, which gives you anti-virus, anti-spam and other security software in one package. It's often cheaper than buying individual products.

It's worth mentioning the open source Thunderbird email program here too: it has built-in junk mail filters, and we've found them to be very effective. The program is free and you can get it for PCs and Macs.

Backup software

It's never a bad idea to prepare for the worst. Good backup software enables you to copy essential documents and data to external hard disks, CDs or DVDs, so if disaster strikes then you haven't lost your important information.

There are lots of good products to choose from. We like Roxio's Easy Media Creator (around £50) for PCs and Toast (again, around £50) for Macs, but if you're buying an external hard disk or other device then don't spend any money on software until you've opened the box: many external hard disks, DVD burners and other storage devices come with free backup software that's perfectly adequate for everyday use.

PDF viewer

Adobe's Portable Document Format, or PDF for short, has become the standard way to publish documents digitally. Computer firms publish their manuals in PDF and government departments provide forms and factsheets in PDF; if you don't have a PDF viewer then you won't be able to open them.

If you've got a Mac, you don't need a stand-alone PDF viewer: Mac OS X has support for PDF files built into the operating system. On PCs, you can get Adobe's Reader program for free from **www.adobe.com/products/acrobat/readstep2.html**.

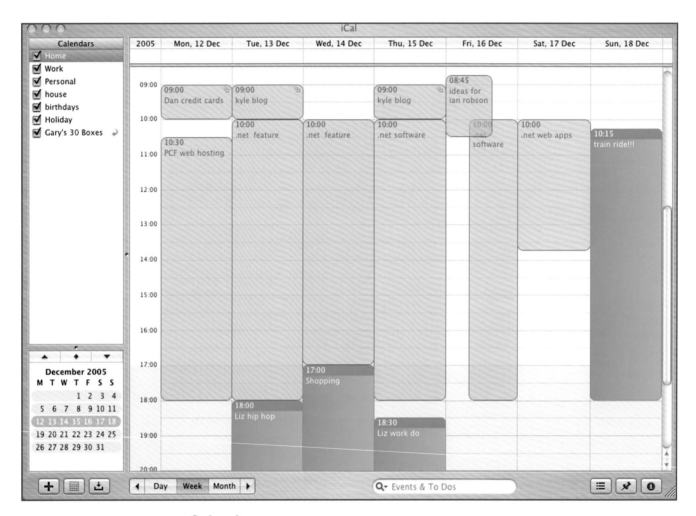

Calendar programs such as Apple's iCal enable you to manage multiple calendars and to synchronise data with external devices such as PDAs.

Calendar

Electronic calendars have one big advantage over paper ones: printed calendars can't sound an alarm to remind you of upcoming appointments or nag you about your to-do list. If you've got a Pocket PC, Palm-powered PDA or smartphone, you can even synchronise calendars between your computer and your PDA or phone, and you can add new appointments when you're out and about. When you return to the office, your PDA or phone can then update your computer's calendar with the new details.

Every new Mac comes with the excellent iCal program, which provides calendar features and a to-do list. If you've got Microsoft Office (or if you buy a Windows-powered Pocket PC or smartphone – Outlook comes as part of the package), then Outlook does a sterling job of organising your life. Alternatively you could use an online calendar such as Yahoo!'s free calendar system (**http://calendar.yahoo.com**), which you can access from any internet-enabled computer.

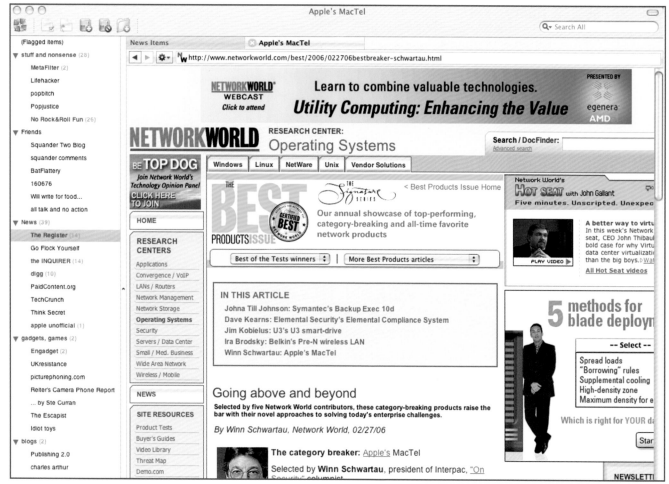

Newsreader

More and more sites now publish their headlines and even entire articles in a format called RSS (which is short for Really Simple Syndication) and newsreader software is designed to access those feeds. It's a very powerful way of keeping on top of your favourite sites: when you find a site you like, subscribe to its feed and then your RSS reader will let you know any time a new story is published. Newsreader software also enables you to flag interesting items so you can refer to them later, or to search your subscriptions for specific subjects.

One of the best PC newsreaders is FeedDemon (**www.bradsoft. com/feeddemon**), which costs around £20; on the Mac, we'd recommend NetNewsWire (**http://ranchero.com/netnewswire**), which is about £15. Alternatively you could use an online newsreader such as Bloglines (**www.bloglines.com**), which is free.

Many web browsers also enable you to subscribe to RSS feeds from sites. Firefox and Safari both support RSS feeds now, and Internet Explorer will add RSS support when version 7 is released in mid-2006.

Newsreader software such as NetNewsWire enables you to 'subscribe' to dozens of different sites. The program then automatically downloads the latest headlines and stories.

Desktop search utility

Once again, Mac users don't need additional software to find files on their machine: OS X's Spotlight feature makes it easy to find anything on your computer. Windows Vista will have similar features built-in, but if you're using an older version of Windows then a free download such as Google Desktop (**http://desktop.google.com**) enables you to Google your own hard disk. Such software can save you a great deal of time, and the more files on your computer the more useful such software becomes.

Zip utility

Many software downloads come in .zip format, which means they've been compressed in order to reduce the overall file size. However zip software isn't just for downloads: you can use it to archive old files and free up hard disk space, or to reduce the size of files when you send them via email or upload them to an internet site. As with most utilities, both PC and Mac owners are spoilt for choice when it comes to compression utilities, and you can get the tools you need for free. If you've got a PC try Camunzip (**www.camunzip.com**); on the Mac, go for Stuffit Expander (**www.stuffit.com**).

Security software

Every few weeks, newspapers report the same story with different names: someone buys a second-hand computer and is stunned to discover that its hard disk contains secret government documents, a corporation's world domination plan, or an individual's secret diary. If you're dealing with sensitive information, it's worth considering security software to hide your data from prying eyes – and to wipe that data when it's time to sell your computer.

Security software typically does one of two things: secure deletion, which gets rid of files permanently and is the electronic equivalent of a document shredder; and encryption, which scrambles your data to make it completely unreadable. Once a file is encrypted, you can only decrypt it if you have the correct identification details, usually a password.

You'll find secure deletion and encryption tools in many off-the-shelf security suites, but you can also get effective tools online for free. For example, Cryptainer LE (**www.cypherix.co.uk/cryptainerle**) provides free encryption for Windows machines that's effectively impossible to bypass. The firm behind the program even makes a version for encrypting files on Pocket PCs.

Tracking software

To fight car crime many vehicles now have electronic trackers, which can locate the car in the event of theft. You can get similar technology for computers, too.

With programs such as PC PhoneHome and Mac PhoneHome (both around £16 from **www.pcphonehome.com**), you can track down your computer if somebody steals it. The idea behind PC

Programs such as Google Desktop make it easy to find files, photos and other important data. If it's on your computer, Google Desktop will find it.

PhoneHome is simple enough. Whenever you're connected to the internet, it sends an invisible email message to the email address of your choice. This message contains the location of the computer and, if your machine has been stolen, the people behind PC PhoneHome can liaise with the police in order to recover your computer.

Some products go even further. Mac tracker Undercover (around £16 from **www.orbicule.com/products/**) doesn't just tell the manufacturers where it is; if the stolen Mac has an iSight camera, it also sends photographs of the thief. Undercover also has a plan B: if it isn't connected to the internet, it simulates a major hardware failure in an attempt to encourage the thief – or oblivious new owner – to take the machine in for repair, at which point Undercover does the electronic equivalent of shouting 'Help! I've been nicked!' to raise the alarm.

Do you need tracking software? If you're using a desktop, probably not: while any computer can be stolen, laptops are much more likely to be misplaced or misappropriated. Most tracking software costs less than £20, and if it successfully recovers a stolen computer then you may feel that £20 is money well spent.

Tracking software such as PCPhoneHome can help you locate a computer in the event of loss or theft.

So far we've explored the furniture, tools and programs you need to make your home office happen – now, it's time to get practical. In Part 4, we'll discover how to put it all together and get your office ready for action.

PART **4**

WORKING FROM HOME MANUAL

Putting it all together

It's time to make your home office a reality. We'll connect up your computers, share your broadband connection via wired and wireless networking, and hook up a photo printer. We'll also look at the ways in which you can make a laptop computer more like a desktop by connecting an external keyboard and mouse and even an external monitor.

For this part, we've used a desktop PC and a notebook PC from Dell, but the steps will be almost identical no matter which manufacturer your computer equipment comes from. There is one exception, though: all-in-one PCs such as Apple's iMac, where the computer and monitor are together in the same case. Setting up such a machine is more like using a laptop: all you need to do is connect the power, broadband, the keyboard and the mouse and you're ready to go.

PUTTING IT ALL TOGETHER

Setting up a desktop PC

The days when desktop computers came as a jumble of boxes and mysterious cables are, thankfully, long gone. However, the constant improvements in technology don't always make life easier: for example, a few years ago keyboards and mice had special, dedicated connectors that were also colour-coded for easy identification. In some cases, the plugs were even specially shaped, which made it impossible to connect the wrong thing to the wrong socket. Now, keyboards and mice are usually USB devices, which means that they all have the same bland, black rectangular plugs. It doesn't make setting up your PC any more difficult, though: it just means you can't identify what's connected to your computer without following the cables to each individual device.

Connecting a flat-panel monitor

Most desktop PCs now come with a flat-panel monitor, which offers several advantages over the traditional cathode ray tube (CRT) monitor. They use less power, they're easier to read, they

don't suffer as badly from reflection or glare and they're much smaller and lighter than equivalent CRT monitors – which means that you don't need a giant desk to make room for them, and you won't get a hernia if you have to move the monitor.

Some flat-panel monitors will arrive fully assembled, but others – like this Dell screen – come in two sections: the display itself and the pedestal on which it sits. Before you put the two pieces together, remove any packaging and make sure you have all of the necessary pieces: the display, the pedestal, the VGA cable (to connect the monitor to the computer) and the power cable. In some cases, you'll find that the power cable is packed with the computer itself, rather than with the flat-panel monitor.

Sit the pedestal upright on your desk and lift the display over it. Be careful – although flat-panel monitors are lighter than their CRT equivalents, they're still fairly heavy. Using two hands, lift the display over the pedestal so the pedestal's mounting plate is lined up with the appropriate space on the back of the display panel.

Tilt the display panel slightly and place it on top of the mounting plate – you'll find it helps to align the display panel with the mounting plate if you can see it, so if you can't peer over the top of the screen then turn the mounting plate away from you. You can then bring the display panel backwards onto the mounting plate. Whichever method you use, insert the top edge of the plate into the back of the display panel. Once you've done this, push the display panel firmly onto the plate until the pedestal locks into place with a satisfying click.

❸

Now, you can connect the VGA cable – it's the cable with two D-shaped connectors and screws to hold the cable in place. VGA connections on flat-panel monitors can be fiddly, and you might find it's easier to connect the cable if you place the display panel face-down on your desk. If, as in this example, your monitor's pedestal has a space for the cables to run through, pass the cable through the gap in the pedestal and then connect it to the D-shaped VGA connector on the display.

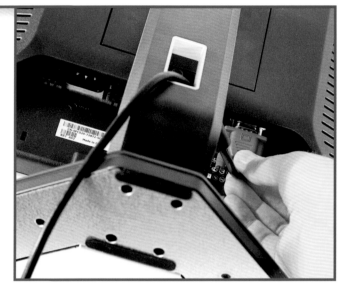

❹

VGA connectors are very fragile: they contain very thin metal pins and those pins are easily bent or broken. That's why VGA cables come with thumbscrews: if you use them to screw the connectors to your monitor and to your PC, it keeps those pins safe from harm. Screwing the connector to the monitor is simple: with a finger and thumb, grab the ridged thumbscrew and turn it clockwise until it's tight.

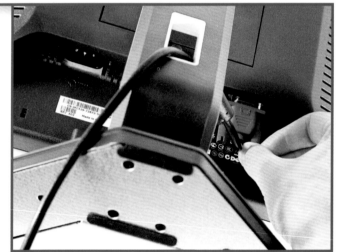

❺

Now, you can connect the power cable, which looks like a kettle lead – but don't plug it into the mains just yet. Feed the small end of the cable through the gap in the pedestal (if your monitor has one) and then plug it firmly but not forcefully into the socket on the back of the display. The socket is usually on the opposite side from the VGA connector, so if the VGA connector is on the left-hand side then the power socket will be on the right.

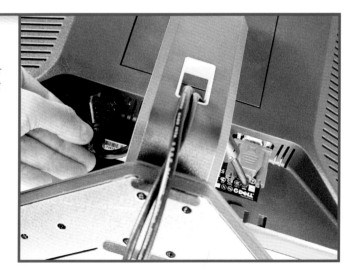

The next step is to adjust the display to get the best viewing angle, but before you do this you should double-check that the display is firmly locked onto its pedestal. If it isn't, when you try to tilt or move the screen it may fall off the pedestal and damage the screen or whatever it falls on. You should also make sure that the VGA and power cables have room to move. If they're too tight, when you attempt to tilt or move the display you could damage the connections on the back of the display panel.

Although it's possible to make a flat-panel monitor completely vertical, it's often better to tilt it back slightly – especially if you're tall, in which case the top of your head will be several inches above the top of the display. To adjust the display angle, hold the pedestal with one hand to keep it in place and, with your other hand, push or pull the bottom edge of the display towards you or away from you.

Preparing the printer

No matter what kind of printer you buy, you'll have to do some simple setting up before you can use it with your computer. If you've bought a laser printer you'll need to install the toner cartridge, which is just a matter of opening up the printer and slotting the cartridge into place. If you've bought an inkjet – and it's likely that you have, because they're the most popular printers in the UK – then the process is slightly more involved. In this walkthrough, we'll use a Dell photo printer, but you'll find the procedure is almost identical for every inkjet. The only key difference you're likely to encounter is the number of ink cartridges: the Dell uses a black cartridge and a colour cartridge, but some printers have three, four or even six colour cartridges.

When you buy a printer, it's worth checking whether it comes with a printer cable: if you don't, you might find that you've set it up perfectly but can't connect it to your computer. If you buy your printer as part of a computer bundle – as was the case with our Dell – then the cable should be included, but if you buy the printer separately then you'll usually have to buy a printer cable as well.

Because printers tend to be fragile and have lots of parts, such as paper trays and output trays, you'll usually find lots of sticky tape on your new printer. This is designed to stop fragile components from moving around in transit, and it's important to remove all of the tape before you insert paper or install the ink cartridges.

In most cases your printer will have two plastic trays: one for putting the paper in, and one for the paper when it comes out. The input tray will also have two plastic guides, which you can move left or right. When you insert the paper, adjust the guides so they're nice and tight against the edges of the paper – but not so tight that the paper bends. This ensures that the paper goes into the printer at the correct angle, so you don't end up with squint prints.

Turn the printer around, locate the power cable and – without connecting the plug end to the mains – insert the small end into the appropriate socket on the back of the printer. Once you've done this, turn the printer around again so you can see the control panel and then plug the power cable into the mains.

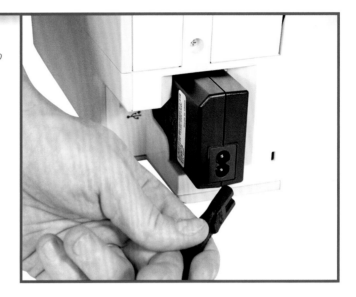

The same printer models are sold in a huge range of countries and, as a result, they can be programmed to work in a range of languages. The first thing you'll see when you connect the power for the first time is a screen asking you to select the display language; in the case of Dell, the default setting is English and pressing the green Start button confirms the setting.

Inkjet printers don't come with their ink cartridges already installed. If they did, the ink would get everywhere during transit and when you opened the box, you'd encounter a horrible mess. The cartridges will be packed inside the printer box, usually in foil or cardboard wrappings and, once you've taken them out of their packaging, the actual installation is easy. First of all, you need to open the printer. Printers are usually hinged at the back and you can open them by lifting from the front, as you can see here.

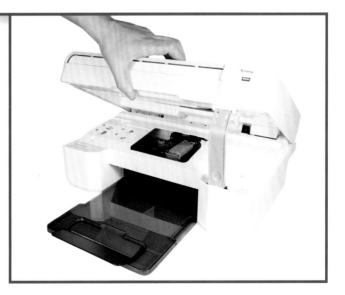

6

Lift the lid of the printer until it locks in place. This means both of your hands are free to install the cartridges. If the printer is on, the cartridge holder should now glide until it sits in the centre of the printer; if it isn't switched on, you'll need to close the lid, switch on the power and then open the lid again.

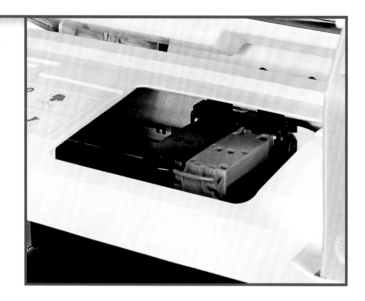

7

Our Dell printer has two cartridge holders: a black one, which is where we'll put the black ink cartridge, and a blue one, which is where the colour cartridge goes. Each holder has a lid that locks in place and keeps the cartridge from moving. To open the lid, press down on the edge nearest you. The lid should now pop up, revealing the space where the ink cartridge will go.

You can now install the black cartridge – but before you do, check the bottom of it for a plastic strip. Most ink cartridges come with such a strip over the print head to stop the ink from escaping in transit. Once you've removed the strip, you can simply push the cartridge into place, pressing down firmly (but not forcefully) to lock it in place.

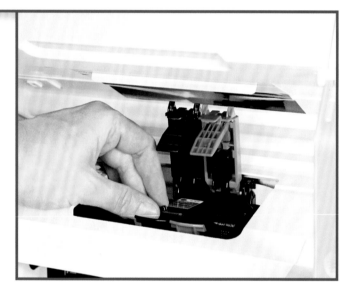

8

Now you can insert the colour cartridge. The process is identical: remove the protective strip from the bottom of the ink cartridge and then press it into place. If your printer uses more than one colour cartridge, make sure you put the right colour cartridge in the right cartridge holder: they are usually colour-coded for easy identification.

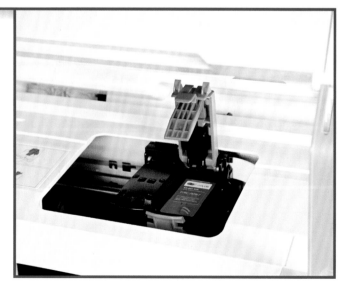

Once the black and colour cartridges are in their holders, the next step is to close the lids to lock them securely in place. To do this, just press the lid of each cartridge holder firmly down until it locks in place with a click. If you have to use force to close the lids, the cartridges haven't been inserted correctly: if that's the case, lift them out and insert them again.

Once the cartridges are locked in place, you can close the printer again. With some printers that's just a matter of pressing down on the lid, but with many printers – including our Dell – there's a locking support strut that holds the printer open. To close the lid, hold it with one hand and with the other, push the support strut backwards until it unlocks. Lower the lid until it clicks into place.

There's one more thing we need to do: align the ink cartridges so that the colour and black inks go where they're supposed to go. On most printers this process is automatic, and our Dell is no exception: when you've installed the ink cartridges and close the lid it tells you to press Start to print a test page. If everything's okay, the printer will print a selection of black, grey and coloured shapes to demonstrate that the cartridges are correctly aligned.

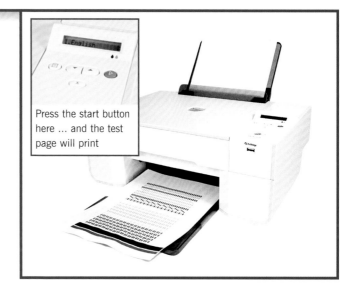

Press the start button here … and the test page will print

You've inserted the paper, connected the power, chosen the language, installed the ink cartridges and printed a test page. All that's left to do is to connect the printer cable. In most cases, the printer cable will be a standard USB printer cable, as shown here. USB printer cables have two different connectors: the familiar, flat, rectangular plug at one end and a smaller, more rounded plug at the other. The smaller plug is the one you should connect to your printer.

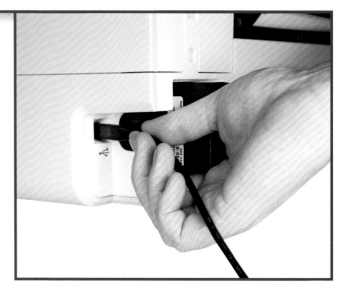

Connecting everything to your computer

The printer's ready and the flat-panel monitor is sitting proudly on your desk. It's time for the easiest bit yet: connecting the keyboard, mouse, monitor and printer to your PC. For the sake of clarity we've taken our photos with the computer sitting on top of our desk, but in a typical home office you can make better use of the available space by placing the computer underneath your desk and running the keyboard, mouse and monitor cables down the back. If you choose this option make sure there's a bit of 'wiggle room' with each cable: if they're too tight, you could damage the connectors.

Most PC peripherals use USB connectors, and many modern PCs have USB ports on both the front and the back of the computer. We'd recommend leaving the ones on the front for things you'll use occasionally, such as digital cameras or music players; for essential things such as your keyboard, your mouse and your printer it's better to use the USB ports on the back of your PC.

When you unpack the keyboard you'll probably find that the keyboard cable is festooned with little plastic cable ties. These keep the cable tidy in the box, but you should remove them before connecting the keyboard to your computer. The keyboard will usually have a USB connector, which you should plug into a free USB port on the back of your PC. It doesn't matter which port you use: each USB port is identical, and there isn't a particular order in which you should connect devices to the USB ports.

Now for the mouse. Again, remove the cable ties and insert the USB plug in the next available USB port. USB connections should slide in easily: if they don't, turn the plug the other way around (USB connectors can only be connected one way). Never try to force a connector into a socket: if you do, you could seriously damage the plug – or even your PC.

TECHIE CORNER

Wireless wonders

Keyboards and mice that cut cable clutter

One of the minor irritations about computer equipment is that the more devices you have, the more your home office resembles Spaghetti Junction. However, a growing number of devices enable you to connect peripherals without wires, and you can even get wireless keyboards and mice.

Wireless keyboards and mice use one of two technologies: Bluetooth is Apple's preferred option for wireless equipment and radio waves are used by manufacturers such as Logitech. Bluetooth devices only work with Bluetooth-enabled computers such as Apple's iMacs, while radio-based cordless devices use a receiver that plugs into a spare USB port. Although Bluetooth is less prone to interference from other devices than

Cordless keyboards and mice such as Logitech's S530 Cordless Desktop can help reduce cable clutter.

radio waves, we've found that there's little practical difference between Bluetooth and radio keyboards: the choice really depends on whether your computer has Bluetooth, and on which particular keyboard and mouse you like the look of.

Too many connections!

Running out of USB sockets? A hub will help.

As we've seen in this part, whether you're connecting a keyboard or a printer you'll need to plug it into a spare USB port. That's fine with a desktop PC, where it's not unusual to have four, six or even eight USB ports, but if you use a laptop you're unlikely to have more than two USB ports. So what happens when you need to connect three, four or even more USB devices?

There are two ways to deal with the problem. Many keyboards and even some monitors come with extra USB ports built-in so, for example, if you have a USB keyboard, you'll often find that it has two additional USB sockets on the back. Alternatively, you could invest in a USB hub. Hubs are simple and cheap bits of hardware that work like four-way electrical sockets: you plug the hub into a USB port on your computer, and it gives you four or more USB sockets for your other hardware.

It's worth noting that some USB peripherals such as Pocket PC cradles, wireless keyboards, USB wireless network adaptors and so on need quite a lot of power, so while they'll work happily if you plug them directly into your computer they can't get enough power when they're sharing a hub with several other devices. You can get round this too, though: you can buy a USB hub that comes with a power supply, which ensures that the hub delivers enough power for the most demanding peripherals.

It's USB time again, but this time we're connecting the printer cable. If you're using a network printer you don't need to connect the printer to your PC; instead, you connect your PC to the network via a router and the printer connects to the router too. We'll look at routers in more detail in a moment.

Ethernet cables connect your PC to your broadband router or to some broadband modems, and you connect the cable as if you were connecting a telephone cable: make sure it's the right way up and press it into the socket until it locks in place with a click. If you're using a stand-alone broadband modem rather than a router, it won't use Ethernet: you connect it to a spare USB port instead.

6

There are only two more cables to go: the VGA cable for the flat-panel monitor, and the power cable for the computer. Connecting the VGA cable to your computer is the same as connecting it to your monitor: make sure the D-shaped connector is the correct way up and then press it onto the D-shaped connector on the back of your PC.

7

Be very careful when you connect the VGA cable: the pins in the connector are easily bent, so it's important to place the cable directly onto the connector rather than approach it from an angle. If the angle is correct you should be able to connect the cable by pushing it firmly but not forcefully into place. Once you've done this, tighten the thumbscrews by turning them clockwise until they're tight (but not too tight).

8

Congratulations: your PC is nearly ready to run. There's only one thing left to do and that's to connect the power cable. Plug the small end into the socket on the back of the PC and make sure it's nice and snug: if it isn't, the cable could move and cut the power to your PC when you're in the middle of something important. Plug the other end into the mains and press the On button on the front of the PC.

9

And that's it: your PC, printer and flat-panel monitor should be up and running. If your printer came with an installation CD, you should use it now: while most USB printers don't need additional software to print basic documents, if you want to take advantage of features such as scanning or if you want to get the best quality prints then you'll need to install the appropriate software.

PART  # Setting up a laptop PC

Laptop PCs are much easier to set up than desktop computers, not least because the screen is already connected to the computer. However, there are potential problems too – and the main one is that laptops have far fewer connectors than desktop PCs. As we'll discover in this walkthrough, that doesn't mean you can't connect all your devices: it just means you need to connect them in a slightly different way.

Laptops are much more flexible than desktop PCs, but there's a price to pay: fewer connections, such as USB ports.

It's a good idea to have a separate keyboard for your laptop, especially if you'll be doing lots of typing while you're in your home office. Some keyboards, such as this Dell one, come with wrist rests that are designed to make keyboarding more comfortable.

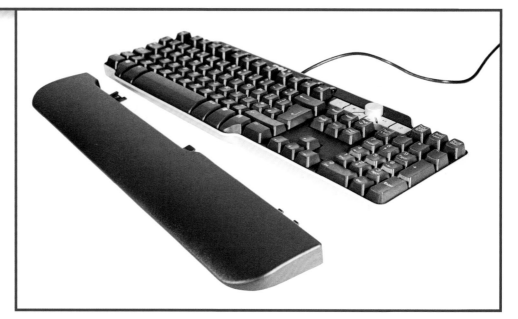

The wrist rest is designed to slot into the front of the keyboard, which will have slots into which the wrist rest can clip. Fitting a wrist rest is easier if you turn the keyboard upside down to reveal the slots, and then line up the clips with the slots.

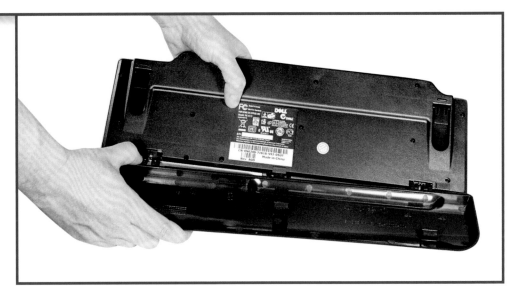

Once you've lined up the clips with the slots, press the wrist rest firmly (but not forcefully: the clips are fragile and if you push too hard you may break them) into place. Depending on the kind of keyboard you have, you might need to squeeze the clips slightly to do this. The wrist rest should now click securely into place.

As with our desktop PC's keyboard, the laptop keyboard needs to be plugged into a spare USB port. Locate the USB ports on your laptop (they'll be at the side or on the back of the case) and slot the keyboard connector into place.

5

The mouse needs to be connected to a USB port too, but rather than use up another of the laptop's precious USB ports we'll use one on the keyboard instead. With our keyboard the USB ports are on the back, but with other models the ports are often on the left and right side of the keyboard case.

6

The quickest way to get your laptop online is to connect it to your router, which is what we've done here. As with a desktop PC, simply plug one end of an Ethernet cable into the computer's Ethernet port and then plug the other end into your router.

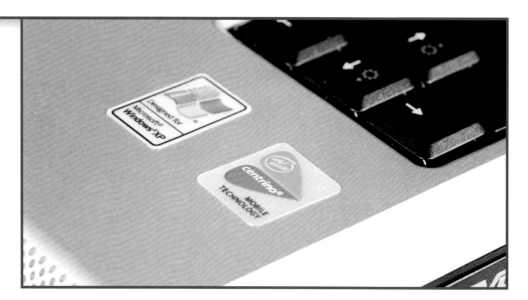

7

The Centrino logo on a laptop means that all the necessary equipment for wireless networking is already inside the machine, so you won't need any additional hardware to take advantage of wireless networks at home or when you're on the move (provided that you have a wireless router that the laptop can connect to!).

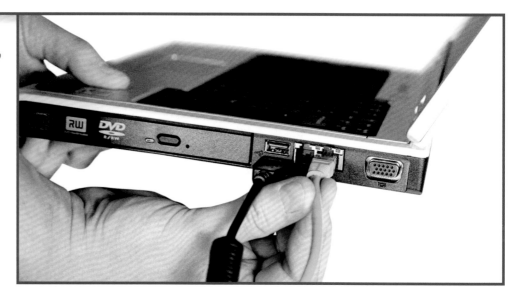

Finally you can connect the power. Although laptops are designed to run on batteries, those batteries don't last long – and if you connect external devices such as keyboards and mice, or if you use wireless networking, the battery life deteriorates further. Plugging the laptop into the mains means the battery's always charged when you want to go mobile.

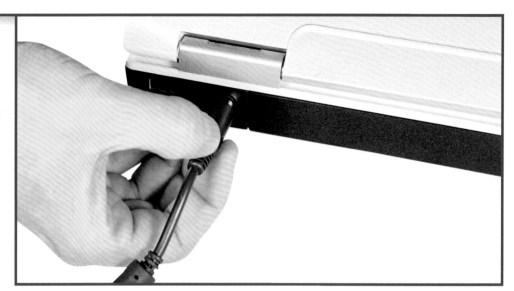

And here's the result: all the benefits of a desktop PC without the bulk. If you'll be using the laptop in your home office for long periods of time, it's worth putting the machine on a laptop stand: this raises the top of the screen to a better height and can help reduce neck strain.

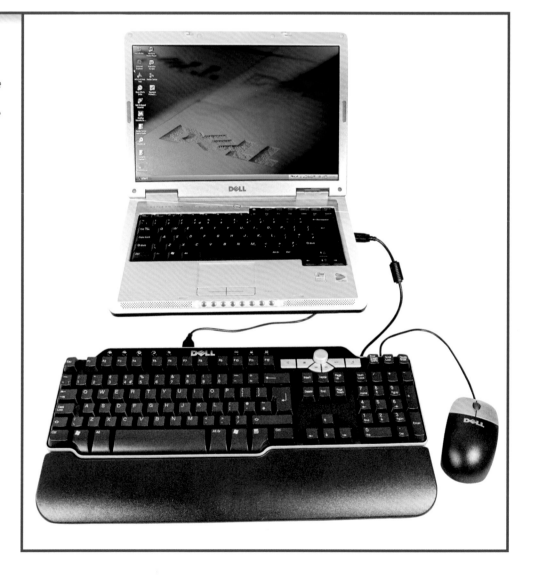

Using an external monitor

Most laptops can be used with an external display so, for example, you could connect a flat-panel monitor when you're in the office or use the laptop as part of a twin-screen setup with the laptop showing one lot of programs and an external monitor showing another lot of programs.

Most laptops have a VGA connector that you can use to connect a display, but it's important to note that they don't all support dual-screen display: many machines, particularly budget machines, use a technique called 'mirroring' instead. That means that what appears on the laptop screen is duplicated on the external display, but you can't display one thing on the laptop and a different thing on the external monitor. Your laptop's manual will tell you whether your machine supports dual display or just mirroring.

Even if your laptop doesn't support dual displays, it might still be worth connecting an external monitor: while laptop screens are rarely larger than 15 inches on mid-range models and 17 inches on the really expensive ones, you could hook up a 19, 20, 26 or even 30-inch flat-panel monitor. That means you could have a laptop with a small 10-inch or 12-inch screen for maximum portability and battery life, but as soon as you returned to your home office you'd have all the benefits of a much bigger monitor.

Connecting an external monitor works in exactly the same way as it does with a desktop PC: simply connect the VGA cable to the VGA port on your laptop, and that's it. Not all laptops have VGA connectors, though, and some machines such as Apple's MacBook Pro use a more modern type of connector called a DVI connector. If your monitor doesn't support DVI you'll need to invest in a DVI to VGA connector, which enables you to connect a VGA cable to your laptop's DVI port.

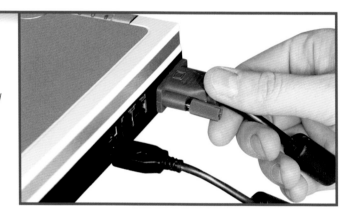

When you connect an external monitor, your laptop should recognise it immediately and begin displaying the screen on the external monitor. If your laptop doesn't support a twin-screen setup it can be distracting to see the same thing on two screens, but you'll find that most machines have a function key on the keyboard that you can use to switch off the laptop screen altogether.

DVI versus VGA

In our tutorial, we connected the computer's screen to the PC using a VGA (video graphics array) cable, which is the standard connection for monitors. However, on many laptop and desktop computers you'll find a different kind of connector, called digital visual interface (DVI). Many desktops come with a DVI and a VGA port, while a growing number of laptops are DVI-only. So what does this mean, and do you need to worry about it?

DVI is a more modern form of connection. VGA cables date back to the days of big and bulky cathode ray monitors, and DVI is designed for today's flat-panel monitor screens. There are two key differences between the standards: they have different types of connectors (so you can't connect a VGA cable to a DVI socket without an adaptor, and vice versa); and VGA uses an analogue signal, while DVI is entirely digital. That means that when you connect a DVI-capable monitor to a DVI port you should get a sharper, more vivid picture with more accurate colour.

That's the theory, but in practice there isn't a great deal of difference until you start using a 30 inch flat-panel monitor, many of which can't be connected to PCs that don't have DVI ports. In some cases, such as Apple's and Dell's 30 inch screens, even one DVI connector isn't enough:

DVI to VGA adapters, such as this one from Amazon.com, enable you to attach your monitor's VGA cable to a DVI port on a PC or laptop. Expect to pay around £10.

to use these monitors, you'll need a graphics card with dual-DVI outputs. Such cards are expensive, and the screens are more expensive still: at the time of writing, a 30 inch monitor costs just under £1,800.

For everyday use, it doesn't matter whether you connect via DVI or VGA, and the only problem you're likely to encounter is when you buy a laptop with no VGA connector at all. To connect a VGA monitor, you'll need a DVI to VGA adaptor, which you attach to the end of your VGA cable and then to the laptop's DVI port. In most cases the laptop manufacturer will include such an adaptor, but if it doesn't you can buy one for around £10 from online shops such as **Dabs.com**.

Why closing a laptop lid can be dangerous

In our photograph we've connected an external display and then closed the laptop lid completely, but that's not always a good idea. Running in 'clamshell mode' as it's called is fine for some machines but not for others, so for example while it's okay to use an Apple PowerBook in clamshell mode it's a bad idea to do the same with an Apple iBook. In extreme cases, running a laptop in clamshell mode could cause the machine to overheat, damaging its circuits or its screen.

The culprit is heat. Because laptops cram a lot of components into a very small space, they often get very hot – and they don't have room for the giant cooling fans you'll find in desktop computers. In some cases, laptops are designed in such a way that excess heat escapes via the keyboard, and if you use them with the lid closed then that excess heat can no longer escape. If you're unlucky, that could mean a cooked computer – and if the machine isn't supposed to run in clamshell mode, you won't be able to get it fixed under warranty. That's why you should always check with the manufacturer: it only takes a moment to check, and it could save you from killing your computer.

Installing a network printer

In our walkthrough, we discovered how to prepare an inkjet printer and how to connect it via USB, but if you'll be using several computers then sharing a printer over your office network might be a better idea. Most printer manufacturers make networked models, and the only real difference between such machines and their USB siblings is that the networked versions include an Ethernet port. To connect the machine it's just a matter of plugging an Ethernet cable between your router and the printer and then installing the manufacturer's software on your PCs.

If you're running multiple Windows XP machines or multiple Macs, you don't necessarily need a printer with its own network port: both Windows XP and Mac OS enable you to share a stand-alone printer with the other machines on your office network without any additional hardware. However, it's worth remembering that any print jobs are sent via the machine the printer is physically connected to, so if that machine's switched off then the printer won't be available to any other machine.

PART  # Connecting to the internet

There's one more thing we need to do: we need to connect your computer to the internet. In this tutorial, we'll use a broadband router, which enables us to share our connection with other PCs. If you're using a USB modem and don't intend to use your broadband connection with more than one computer, you can skip this section.

The first step is to connect the broadband cable, which looks like a telephone cable, to the back of the router. If you're using ADSL broadband, the connect the other end to a microfilter – a box that splits your phone line into two connections, one for the phone and the other for the broadband – which plugs into the phone socket. Without a microfilter, you'll lose your internet connection whenever you use the phone.

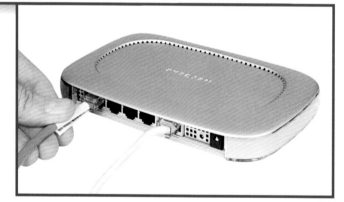

Now, you can connect your PC. We've already connected an Ethernet cable to the back of the PC, and it's just a matter of plugging the other end of the cable into one of the empty Ethernet ports on the back of the router.

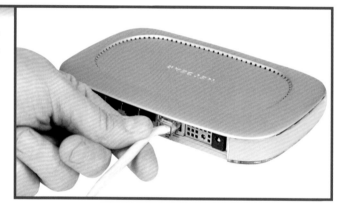

If you'll be sharing your broadband connection, you can do it with an Ethernet cable (as shown here): simply get a second cable, plug one end into the PC and plug the other end into the next available Ethernet port on the router. If you've got a wireless router and will be connecting your other devices via wireless, you can skip this step.

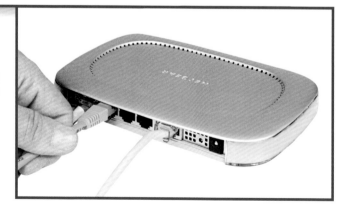

If you've got a third or fourth computer to connect or a networked printer, it's time for yet another Ethernet cable. Once your various computers are connected, you can connect the power cable. It's a good idea to keep the router and its various cables out of harm's way: trailing cables can be a trip hazard, and a good tug on a cable could damage it, the router or whatever else the cable is connected to.

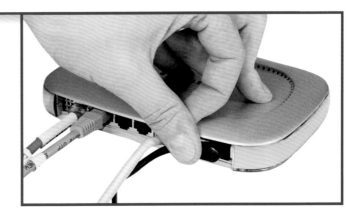

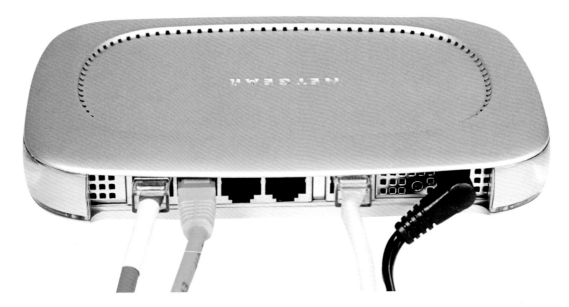

TECHIE CORNER

What is a microfilter?

The little box you need for broadband

With ADSL broadband, your phone and your internet connection share the same phone line – but if you connect your phone and your computer using a standard splitter plug, you'll lose your internet connection any time you make or receive a telephone call.

A microfilter prevents this from happening and ensures that your phone and your internet connection can co-exist peacefully. When you sign up for broadband, your ISP will usually provide at least one such filter, but if it doesn't you can buy microfilters from any high street or online electronics shop. If you have more than one phone connected to the same line that delivers your broadband, you'll need a microfilter for each phone socket. The good news is that they aren't expensive: you can get microfilters for around £3 each.

Microfilters keep your phone line and broadband connection separate, so you won't lose your internet connection every time the phone rings.

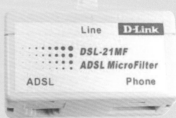

Configuring your router for broadband

Before you can use your router, you need to configure it. For most routers – wired or wireless – you do that via your web browser. The good news is that it's very quick and very easy to do, as we'll discover in this walkthrough.

Once you've connected your cables and plugged in the power cord, boot up your PC and open your web browser. To access the router configuration screen, you'll need to type its address into your web browser. The router manual will tell you what this address is: in this example we're using a Netgear router and the address we have to type is **http://192.168.0.1**.

The router will ask for a user name and password, and once again you'll find these details in the manual. With Netgear routers, the default username is 'admin' and the default password is 'password', so if you enter those details in the appropriate boxes you'll be able to access your router's control panel. Remember to change the user name and password later, or anybody will be able to log in and change your settings!

The control panel looks like a typical web page with a range of categories along the left-hand side of the screen. The first thing we need to do is to configure the router to work with our broadband connection. You'll need your ISP's login details and connection settings to do this, so make sure you've got them handy before attempting this step. Once you've got the necessary details to hand, click on Basic Settings in the left-hand side of the screen.

Every manufacturer takes a slightly different approach, but the principles are the same: you'll be asked whether your connection requires a login (most do) and then for your username and password. You'll also be asked to specify the encapsulation type – your ISP will have given you this information – and to specify your internet IP address and Domain Name Server addresses. In most cases the correct options will be 'Get Dynamically from ISP' and 'Get Automatically from ISP', and your ISP will have provided the necessary numbers if that isn't the case. Finally, you need to select whether Network Address Translation should be enabled; again, in most cases the answer is yes.

Don't worry about the various acronyms – DNS, NAT and so on. All you need to do is to ensure that the information you enter into the router control panel matches the details you've been given by your internet service provider!

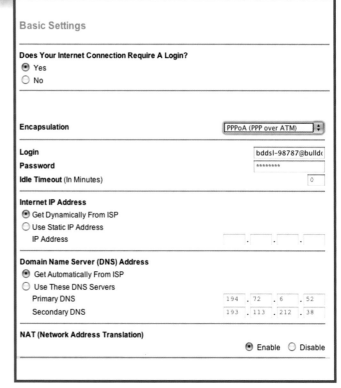

Once you've entered the details, click on Apply to save them permanently. The router will attempt to connect to your broadband connection using the details you've specified; a Netgear router will display a pop-up window that provides a progress report on how it's getting on. If the information you've entered is correct, after a few seconds the pop-up window will change and display the 'success page' shown here. You're up and running!

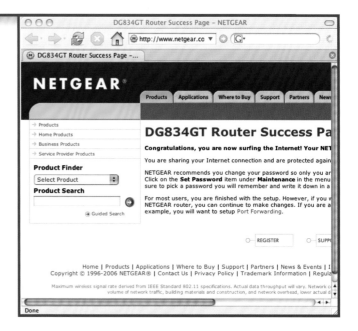

Configuring a wireless network

If you're using a wired router, you can now connect your PCs to the internet without any more changes. If you want to connect PCs to the router over a wireless connection, though, you need to specify a few more details.

Click on Wireless Settings and in the Name (SSID) box, choose a descriptive name for your network such as 'my home office'. Make sure that Enable Wireless Access Point and Allow Broadcast of Name (SSID) are ticked: if they aren't, then your computers won't be able to find the wireless network. These options tell the router that it should let computers connect to it, and that it should broadcast a message that essentially says 'hello! I'm a wireless network and my name is "my home office"'

Now to make your wireless network secure. Click on the WEP (Wired Equivalent Privacy) button to enable the WEP security system, and then choose '128 bit' from the Encryption Strength field. This makes it very difficult for people to get into your network. Now, you need to create a security key. In the Passphrase box, type any phrase you like; the router will then generate a complicated password, called a 'key', such as 9588BEF5DD4... and so on. Take a note of this number: you'll need to enter it on any computer that will use your wireless network. Click on Apply to save the settings.

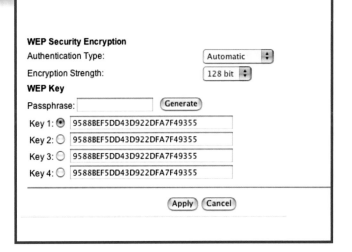

Whenever a wireless-enabled computer is within range of your network, it will spot 'my home network' and ask if it should connect to it. This is where the key you wrote down in Step 7 matters: without it, a computer won't be able to connect to the network (this is a good thing, because it keeps other people's computers out of your network). In this screenshot, we're connecting with an Apple computer: because we've entered the correct wireless key; when we click on OK, we'll be connected to the network.

Wireless security: making sense of the alphabet soup

In our walkthrough we used WEP (Wired Equivalent Privacy) to prevent unauthorised computers from joining our wireless network. However, it's not the only standard, and while all wireless equipment supports WEP, more recent hardware supports even stronger security standards. The two standards you'll see most often are WPA-PSK (Wi-Fi Protected Access Pre-Shared Key) and WPA-802.1x. But what are they?

WPA-PSK is a stronger form of security that's specifically designed for small office and home users. While it's more secure than WEP, it works in essentially the same way: to connect to your network, computers will need to support WPA-PSK security and know the correct network key. The main difference between WEP and WPA-PSK is that the latter is a bit harder for villains to break into. WPA-802.1x is tougher still, but it's really designed for big companies and is intended to be used with a computer server that checks whether computers should be allowed to connect to the network.

Whether you use WEP or WPA-PSK, it's worth considering an access list that turns your router into an electronic bouncer: if your name's not on the list, you don't get in. With most wireless networks, any computer can connect as long as it knows the correct key, but for added security you can create a 'guest list' of machines. If a computer isn't on the list, it can't connect to the network – even if it has the correct key. To set up an access list, you'll need to know the media access control (MAC) addresses of the computers. These are twelve-digit numbers, usually broken up by colons for easier reading. For example, the MAC address of our current computer is 00:0d:93:7e:e1:de.

Finding the MAC address

Finding the MAC address of your computer is very simple, but the process is slightly different on different types of computers. Here's how to find it.

On a Windows 2000 or Windows XP PC
Connect to your wireless network and then click on the Start button. Select Run and in the dialog box that appears, type 'cmd' (without the inverted commas) and press Return. In the small black window that appears, type 'ipconfig /all' (again, without the inverted commas) and look for the bit that says Physical Address. That's your PC's MAC address.

On an Apple Mac
Connect to your wireless network and then open System Preferences > Network. Click on Airport and then on the Configure button. Your Mac's MAC address will be displayed in the form 'AirPort ID: 00:0d:93:7e:e1:de' (the actual numbers will differ from computer to computer).

On a Pocket PC
To find your MAC address, enable wireless networking and

connect to the wireless network. The specific procedure then depends on the type of Pocket PC you have, but in most cases you need to click Start > Settings > Connections and then locate the wireless network manager software – which, handily, is usually called something like Wireless Network Manager, WLAN Utility or something similar. You'll find the MAC address in the Advanced tab.

Creating an access list

Once you've noted the MAC addresses of your computers, creating the access list is very simple. Once again we'll use a Netgear router, but other manufacturers' routers work in much the same way. Use your web browser to open the router's control panel and then click on Wireless Settings. Now, click on the Setup Access List button.

To prevent other machines from accessing your network simply click the Turn Access Control On button and then use Add New Station Manually to enter the details of the computers you want the router to talk to. For example, to add our laptop we'd type 'Laptop' in the Device Name box and 00:0d:93:7e:e1:de in the MAC Address box.

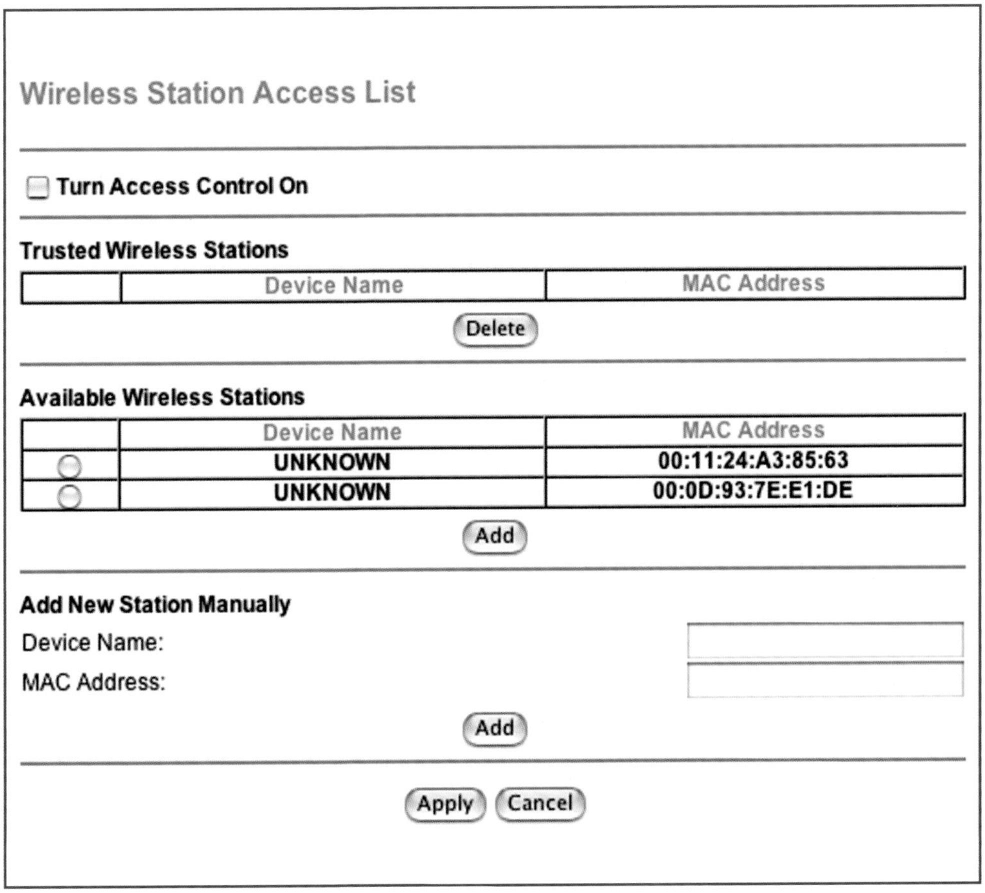

Wireless Station Access List

☐ **Turn Access Control On**

Trusted Wireless Stations

	Device Name	MAC Address

(Delete)

Available Wireless Stations

	Device Name	MAC Address
○	UNKNOWN	00:11:24:A3:85:63
○	UNKNOWN	00:0D:93:7E:E1:DE

(Add)

Add New Station Manually

Device Name:
MAC Address:

(Add)

(Apply) (Cancel)

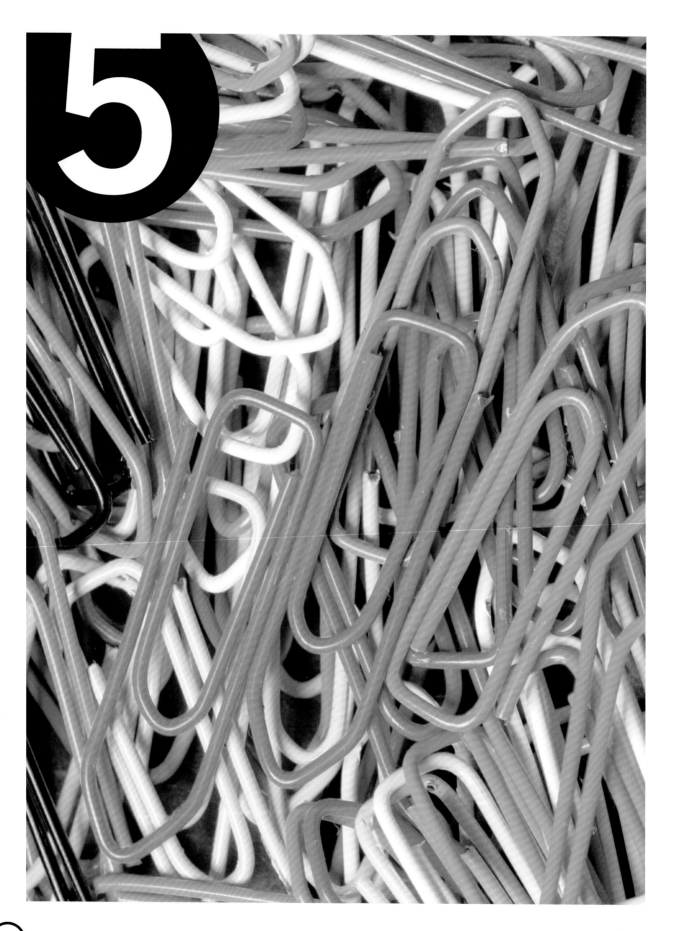

5

WORKING FROM HOME MANUAL

Collaboration

Although you'll be working from home you still need to collaborate with others, whether that means communicating with clients or working on projects with distant colleagues. If you're homeworking on behalf of an employer the firm will usually provide the necessary software, but if you're on your own then the software or service you use is largely up to you.

We'll look at three kinds of software that can make collaboration – and if you're self-employed, networking – child's play: communications software that you can use to keep in touch with clients and colleagues; scheduling software that you can use to prevent calendar conflicts; and software that enables groups of people to work on the same documents simultaneously, or to review each others' input.

PART **5**

COLLABORATION

It's good to talk

The simplest form of communications software is chat software, such as MSN Messenger, AOL Instant Messenger, iChat and so on. These programs enable you to chat in real time with others, and they're all available for free – so, for example, you can download MSN Messenger from Microsoft's MSN site, AOL Instant Messenger from AOL.com, and if you've got a Mac then the iChat AV software is already on your computer.

Chat software doesn't just enable you to type messages in real-time to other people, though: most chat programs also support voice chat, file transfers and in some cases, even video chat. For example, Apple owners can attach a small camera to their computer and then use iChat AV for high-quality videoconferencing with up to three people, although for best results you'll need a speedy broadband connection.

There's one big problem with chat software, though, and that's incompatibility: for example if you're on MSN and your colleagues use iChat AV, you won't be able to communicate with them. You don't have to install multiple chat programs, though: you can use a free multi-chat program such as Trillian (**www.trillian.cc**), which can connect to multiple chat networks simultaneously. It's very clever and very handy, although it's important to note that you'll still need to sign up for free accounts with whatever chat services you want to use – so for example if you want to use Trillian with MSN Messenger, you'll need to sign up for an MSN Messenger account; if you want to use it with Yahoo! Messenger, you'll need a Yahoo! ID, and so on. You'll also find that while Trillian can handle the basics of each chat system, some of the more advanced features won't work – so while it can connect to

Programs such as Trillian solve the problem of incompatibilities between different chat software: the program enables you to use several different chat networks simultaneously.

iChat, it can't handle videoconferencing unless you pay for the more powerful Pro version.

Incompatibility is a huge problem with chat software, and to their credit the various firms who offer chat systems are trying to find ways to make the differing systems work together. However, so far progress has been very slow and you're left with two main choices: persuade everyone you know to use the same chat network that you do, or get a multi-chat client such as Trillian.

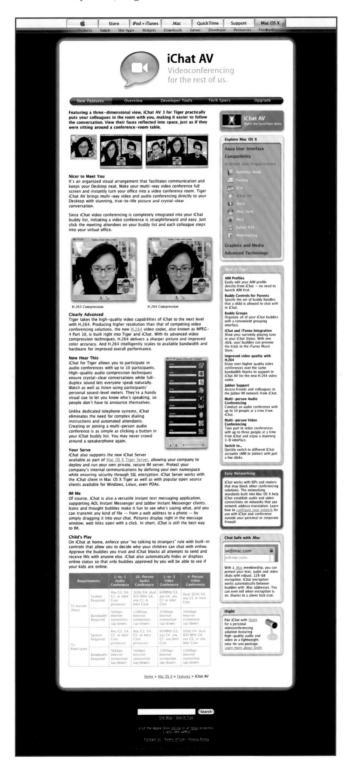

If you've got an Apple Mac and a broadband connection, you can use Mac OS X's iChat AV software for text, voice and even video chat.

COLLABORATION

Message boards and email lists

If you're self-employed, it's often good to talk with other people in your industry. You can share contacts or warn one another of bad clients, get advice from people with more experience, compare rates or just rant and rave about the ups and downs of self-employed life. There's a huge range of message boards and discussion lists for specific industries; for example, journalists talk about their trade at the JournoBiz forums (**www.journobiz.com**), web designers communicate by email at Freelancers.net (**www.freelancers.net**), people in the electronic publishing industry talk shop at ePubPros (**epubpros.chrisknight.com**) and so on.

The main difference between message boards and email lists is that you view the former in your web browser, while with email lists you get a copy of every message sent to the list (and every email you send to the list is copied to all the list members). However, the lines between the two kinds of forum are often blurred, and many email lists are also archived on the web – especially if they use services such as Yahoo! Groups (**http://groups.yahoo.com**).

If you want to set up an email list of your own, Yahoo! Groups is a good place to start. It's very easy to use, it doesn't cost any money and you can decide whether your email list will be open to anyone or to a select group of colleagues, friends or like-minded souls. It also provides additional features such as a file and photo library where you and other list members can upload files and photos, a calendar feature to keep track of upcoming events, polls to gauge people's opinions, and a shared links library where list members can post interesting web links.

Creating an email discussion list

Go to **http://groups.yahoo.com** and click on 'Start a Group Now' at the bottom of the screen. If you've registered with Yahoo! before you'll be asked to log in; if you haven't, you'll be asked to register. Registration doesn't take long and doesn't cost anything, but you won't be able to create a group if you haven't gone through the registration process.

To create a group, you need to tell Yahoo! what kind of group it is. We're creating a group for homeworkers, so we've chosen the category 'Business & Finance'; Yahoo! now asks us what kind of Business & Finance group we're building. The most appropriate category for us is 'Employment and Work', so we'll click on that.

Once you've chosen a category, click on the Start your Group button. You'll now be asked to give your group a name and an email address. The address is where people will send their mailing list messages, and it will automatically end with '@yahoogroups.com'. Once you've entered these details, add a description of your group and click Continue.

Now you need to specify what email address any list messages should be sent to (if you choose the option to receive messages by email rather than to view them on the web). You'll also be asked to type in the letters and numbers you see on screen. This is to prove to Yahoo! that you're a real person. Click Continue when you've done this.

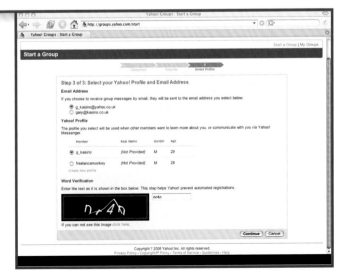

Congratulations: you've created your group. The screen shows you the address of your group's new home page, and the email address for sending messages to the group. Now, it's time to customise the group to specify who can use it and what features will be available. Click on 'Customize Your Group' to do this.

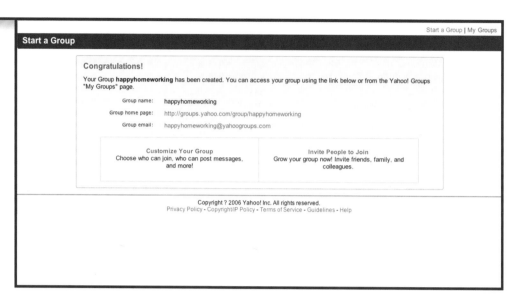

The first step is to decide whether your group will be available to anyone, or whether you want to approve potential new members. You can also specify whether anyone can post messages, or if messages will be members-only. There's a third option, 'Only Group Owner': use this if you want to use your group as an electronic newsletter rather than a forum for debate.

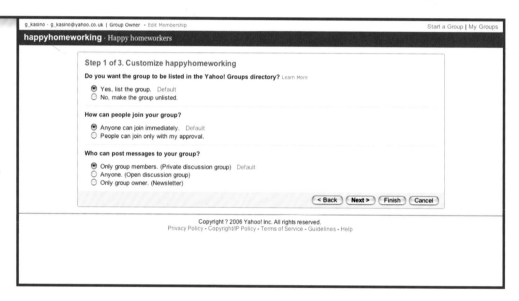

Now you can choose whether to approve each message before it's distributed (rarely a good idea with busy discussion lists) and whether the group will take advantage of Yahoo! Groups' online features. The web features are switched on by default, but you can disable them on this screen if you wish. For now, we'll leave them on.

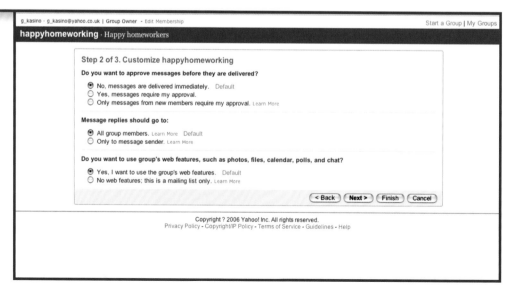

You can now specify who can use the specific features of your group, such as online chat, file and photo sharing, the calendar and so on. You can also specify whether the list archives are public (which means anyone can read old messages), members-only or your eyes only. If you prefer, you can tell Yahoo! not to archive the messages at all.

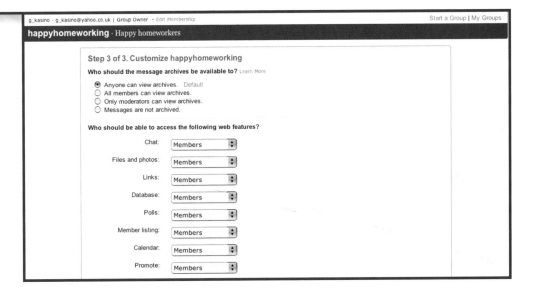

Once you've specified how your group will operate, it's time to add new members. To do this, simply click the Invite link on the left-hand side of your screen. Now you can enter the addresses of the people you'd like to invite. You can either enter their Yahoo! user IDs (if they have such things) or their email addresses.

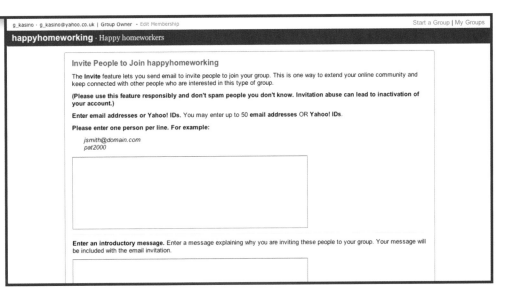

And that's it: you've set up your discussion list and it's just a matter of waiting for people to reply to your invitations and join up. Once they've done that, you can start chatting, uploading files, sharing interesting links or anything else you feel like doing.

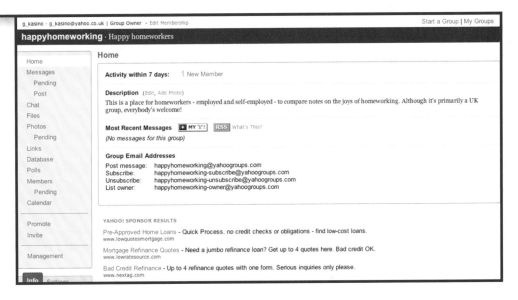

COLLABORATION

Calendar collaboration

As we discovered in Part 3, a calendar program can be a big help when it comes to keeping track of projects and appointments. However, it can also help you collaborate with others and avoid scheduling conflicts. For example, Apple's iCal program can publish calendars online for other iCal users to download, and web-based calendar systems such as the free 30boxes service (**http://30boxes.com**) make it easy for you to publish a calendar online so that others can see when you're available – and when you aren't.

30boxes (and similar services) works just like a normal calendar program, but it also enables you to specify whether others can see your calendar and what bits they can see. For example you can label personal appointments as 'private' so only you can view them; to others, the private appointments will just show up as times when you aren't available. If you prefer, you can specifically label work appointments as 'work' and then only share that part of your calendar with others. If you wish, you can even enable others to add their own appointments to your calendar, so for example a colleague could pencil in a meeting at a time when both of you appear to be free.

One of our favourite 30boxes features is also one of the simplest to use: if you schedule an appointment and then put the appointment address in square brackets, 30boxes automatically links to a Google Map of that address – so if we typed 'Important meeting [Hillington Innovation Centre, Glasgow UK]' in our calendar then 30boxes finds it on Google Maps and creates a link to the map. The link doesn't just provide a map, though: it can also provide driving directions, which can save you a lot of time and effort when you're going to a meeting (or save clients or colleagues a lot of time and effort when they're coming to visit you).

Calendar software such as 30boxes enables you to publish your diary online and, if you wish, you can enable others to view your appointments and even pencil in new ones.

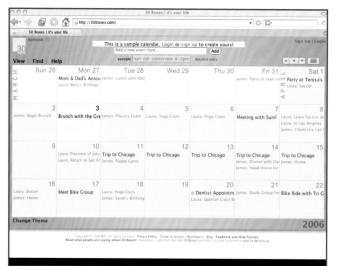

One particularly useful feature of 30boxes is its maps: if you put an address in square brackets in your calendar, it automatically links to a Google Map showing how to get to that address.

PART 5

Document collaboration

There's more to collaboration than sharing calendars and having the odd chat. Sharing documents is an increasingly important element of homeworking, whether you're reviewing someone else's document or working together on a big project such as a brochure or report. The simplest form of such collaboration is to email the document back and forth, but a number of programs have more sophisticated features that can make collaboration easier.

Two of the best programs for collaboration are Microsoft Word and Adobe Acrobat. When you send a document from either program to a colleague or client, they can make changes or add comments – but if you've enabled the document-review features, the software keeps the original document as well as the changes. That means the person with the final say on a document can decide which changes to accept and which ones to reject, and it also means that no matter how many changes you make you can always go back to your first draft.

In order to use Word's review features it's just a matter of selecting Track Changes from the Tools menu. If the other people working on your document also use Word, then it will maintain the original while recording changes. With Acrobat, at least one of you will need a full copy of the Acrobat program, but the other recipients only need the free Acrobat Reader program, which is available for Windows and Mac OS X.

Although document-review features are very useful, unless everyone involved in a project uses the same network then it does still involve a lot of email exchange, with the same document whizzing back and forth between different people. A new breed of collaboration programs aims to change that. Programs such as Writely (**www.writely.com**) run in your web browser, and while they can save documents to your hard disk they're really designed to store documents on the internet. Instead of endless emails you simply put the document on the internet, tell your colleagues or clients where to find it, and they can make changes or add comments from within their web browser – so they don't need to be using the same software as you. As we'll discover in the next walkthrough, Writely is no substitute for Microsoft Word – but if you need an easy way to collaborate with others, it's surprisingly powerful.

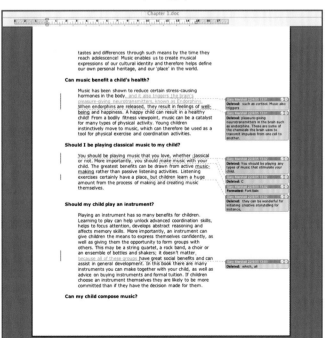

Microsoft Word can track changes to a document, so you can see which bits of the document another person has deleted and which bits they've added.

Using Writely.com

Writely (**www.writely.com**) is a great example of what you can do with nothing more complex than a web browser. It's fast, flexible and free, and it's perfectly suited to simple document creation, editing and collaboration. It's Word-compatible but it's no Word clone: the formatting is much more limited, you don't get all the advanced features you'll find in Microsoft's famous editor and it doesn't include some of the things – Word Count, footnotes and so on – that many Word users find essential. However, it's not supposed to be an Office rival; it's designed to make collaboration easier, and it does that job very well. It's no wonder that search giant Google quickly snapped up the service to add it to its portfolio of products.

Writely was in the middle of moving to Google's systems as this manual went to the printers, so the service may look slightly different from the screenshots shown here. However, the process of creating and sharing your documents with others will remain the same.

The Writely sign-up process is refreshingly simple: instead of endless questions about your house, your job and your pets, it's just a matter of heading over to **www.writely.com***, entering your email address and picking a password. Once you've done this you'll get an email containing a link; you click on the link and the registration process is complete.*

Once you've registered and signed in, you'll see the main Writely screen as shown in our screenshot. The Tour link at the top right of the screen takes you through the basics of using the service, or you can get stuck in by creating or uploading a document. Click New to start working with Writely.

3

A pop-up window will appear, asking you to give your document a name (you might need to disable pop-up-blocking in some browsers to see it). Choose a descriptive name and then click on OK. We won't add collaborators – people who can view and edit your document – just yet.

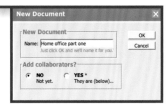

4

You'll now see the main editing window, which looks like a cross between Microsoft Word and Blogger. You can work in two ways: by using the normal editing window, which is a What You See Is What You Get (WYSIWYG) editor, or by clicking on the HTML link to view the document's underlying code.

5

If you're used to word-processing software then it's probably best to stick with the WYSIWYG mode, as we've done in this screenshot. The toolbar provides quick access to common features including the spell checker, the undo and redo commands and the print function. Click on Preview at any time to see the results.

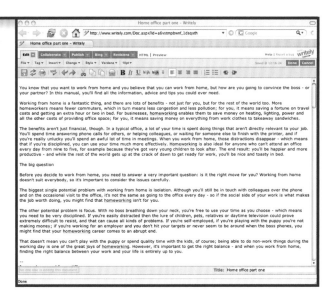

In WYSIWYG mode, formatting works exactly as you'd expect. For example, to turn some text into a bulleted list simply highlight it and then click on the Bullets icon in the toolbar. You can also change the font and size (there aren't many fonts to choose from, though, just the web basics such as Arial, Tahoma, and so on).

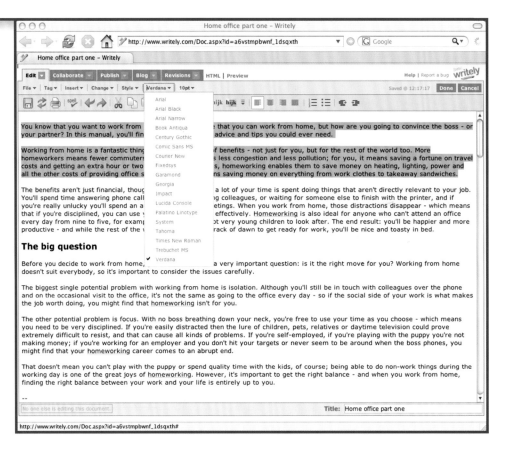

The Insert button on the toolbar is a drop-down menu, and it enables you to add extra elements such as hyperlinks, images, horizontal lines and bookmarks. You can also insert an HTML table, and use the Change menu to adjust its properties if you need to tweak the layout or add more rows or columns.

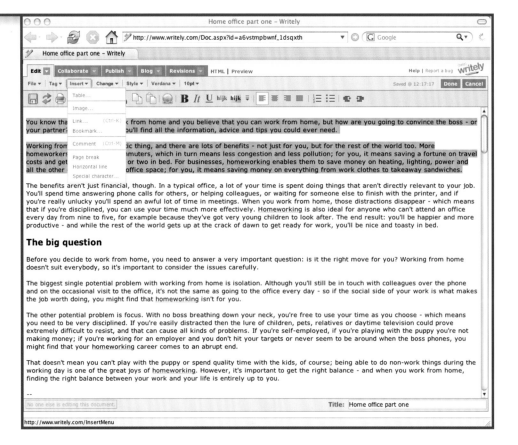

Clicking on the Done button saves your document within Writely, but you can also export it in three main ways: as a Word file, as a Zip file or as an RSS feed. To do this, click on the Actions button towards the top right of the window and choose the export option you want to use.

Click on Done to return to the main Writely screen. One useful feature of this screen is the ability to tag documents, so for example you might want to label some documents as work and others as personal. To do this, tick the box next to the document and select the appropriate option from the Actions menu.

Writely's collaboration features are very easy to set up. Click on the Collaborate tab towards the top left of the window and you'll see the helpful advice shown here. Collaborators aren't the same as viewers: not only will they be able to see your document, but they'll be able to edit it too.

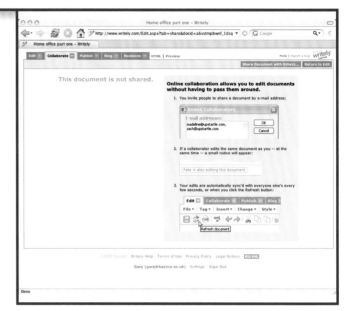

Click on Add Collaborators and a pop-up should appear. Type the email addresses of the people you'd like to add, and then click on OK. Collaborations are on a per-document basis, so you don't need to worry whether your work collaborators will also be able to see love letters, angry rants or other personal documents.

You can add or change collaborators at any time and decide when to contact them. If you're ready for others to take a look at your work, click on OK; if you'd rather wait, click Cancel and then return to the Collaboration tab when you're ready. We're happy to proceed, so click on OK.

Each collaborator will receive an email from Writely that includes a link to the document and a temporary password (they'll be asked to change the password when they login). You can also enter your own text, which will appear in the email; it's a good idea to do this, especially if your collaborators haven't used Writely before.

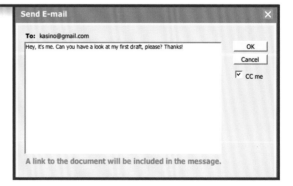

Your collaborators can now log in and add, edit or delete bits of your document, change the formatting and generally muck around with your masterpiece. Each edit is saved, and any changes will be highlighted when you view them. Our screenshot shows a minor document edit; you can see earlier versions by clicking the button marked Older.

Once everyone's had their say and you've come up with a final version, you can save your work and publish it online. You can make the document available to everybody online, or only to a select few; if you go for the latter option, only the people whose email addresses you specify will be able to see your work.

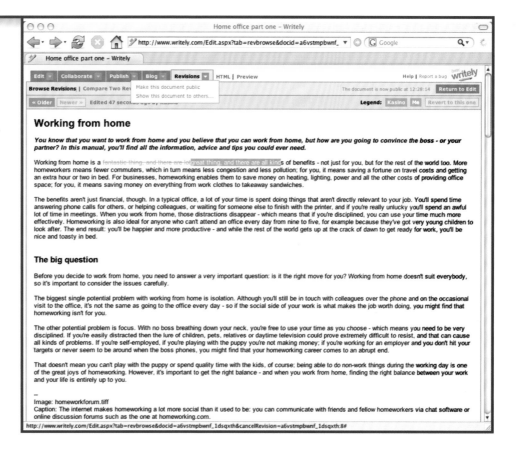

COLLABORATION

Digital discussions: the dangers

Chat software, message boards and email lists are amazingly useful things, but it's important to remember that in many cases your messages will be archived somewhere – potentially forever. Some mailing list archives are freely viewable on the web, which means that a Google search could locate them; others might not be publicly archived, but individual members may hang on to messages they find particularly interesting. The same applies to chat software, too: people who use Google's chat service automatically keep a copy of the chat unless they've switched that feature off, and most chat software enables you to save a copy of the conversation for future reference.

You can never be sure whether your supposedly private discussion is being recorded, so it's very important to think about what you're saying, and to be careful about the people you say it to. As the cliché goes, you should never say anything on the internet that you wouldn't say to someone's face – or that you wouldn't be able to defend in court. Don't assume that you can be

Ellen Simonetti was fired from her job as an airline attendant because her employer felt her personal site brought the company into disrepute.

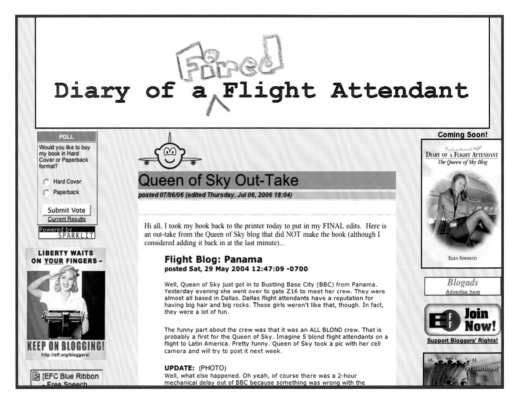

anonymous on the internet, either: in recent years a number of people who blogged anonymously about their employers discovered that they weren't as anonymous as they thought they were. In at least two cases, people have been sacked for writing unfavourable things about their employers online – an employee of Waterstone's bookshops in the UK and a Delta Airlines stewardess in the US.

It's tempting to call clients names or say bad things about the boss, but libel laws apply online as well as in the real world, so if you damage someone's reputation then you could end up in court. Of course, most of us are sensible enough to watch what we post to message boards, discussion lists or blogs' comments sections, but even if you watch what you say and to whom you can still get into trouble. The following disasters have happened to us:

Send ... oops!

Some discussion lists can be lively places, and the busier the list the more likely you are to find someone you disagree with. That happened to us, and after a few days of arguing we wrote a personal email to a friend that said some very unpleasant things about a mailing list member. Unfortunately, we sent the message not to the friend, but to the mailing list in question – which meant that our supposedly private message landed in the inboxes of all 250 list members, including the person we were talking about. As the list is archived online, our slip of the keyboard is permanently available online (much to our embarrassment).

Just because you're paranoid ...

We sent a friendly warning to a journalists' email list about a particularly colourful character who had started calling various newspapers and magazines. The gentleman in question was convinced there was a big conspiracy involving the government, the security services, journalists, JobCentres and pretty much every organisation in the world, and as our warning pointed out, he was a dogged type: if he thought a writer didn't believe him, then he would decide that the writer was part of the conspiracy. He would then embark on a campaign of harassment against the writer, sending hundreds of abusive emails and making dozens of abusive phone calls every day for several weeks.

We warned other writers, but we didn't realise that the message would be permanently archived online – and we didn't realise that the person we were warning other writers about regularly put his own name into Google to see what people were saying about him. Inevitably, he found our message, decided we were part of the conspiracy, and spent the next few weeks emailing and calling not just us, but everyone we've ever worked with.

The moral? If an email, message board post or comment on a website could come back and bite you, don't send it. If an email could cause upset or even trouble if it fell into the wrong hands, don't write it. Murphy's Law applies: the more damaging your comments about someone, the more likely they are to find those comments.

6

PART 6

Security

Murphy's Law famously states that if anything can go wrong, it will. If Murphy had been a homeworker, he would have added 'and it will go wrong spectacularly, and at the worst possible time.' If something were to happen to your important data – or even worse, your computer – the consequences could be disastrous.

Planning for disaster is a bit like having home insurance: you hope you'll never need it, but if something bad happens then you'll thank your lucky stars for it. For homeworkers, disaster planning comes in three key areas: hardware security, data security and disaster recovery.

PART  Hardware security

Securing your computer hardware isn't difficult or
expensive, and in most cases it only requires a few
simple precautions. Wherever possible, computer
equipment shouldn't be visible from outside your home
(we drove past a flat the other evening and could clearly
see a top-of-the-range Apple iMac worth at least £1,300
in the front room; as it was a ground floor flat with big,
single-glazed windows it would be incredibly easy to
break in and steal the computer). It's also worth
investing in a computer-locking system such as a
Kensington Microsaver lock (**www.kensington.com**). This
attaches your computer to a heavy object such as a desk,
and it's very difficult to break or cut.

If you're going to be away from home regularly, installing a
decent alarm system can act as a further burglar deterrent; it's
also a good idea to hide your computer equipment – or even
better, leave it with a relative while you're away. The more
difficult you make life for burglars, the less likely they are to steal
your equipment.

If you've got a laptop, you need to be particularly wary. If you
leave your laptop on a car seat and it gets stolen, your insurance
probably won't pay out: with most policies, valuable items such
as laptops must be locked securely and out of sight in the boot or
you're not covered. Even if you're in the car, it's a bad idea to put
your laptop on a car seat, for two reasons. Firstly, it's easy for
someone to open the door and grab your computer while you're
sitting at traffic lights; secondly, emergency braking could turn

A good-quality notebook case can
protect your laptop from everyday
knocks and bumps, and it doubles
as a briefcase for carrying
documents and other business
essentials.

your laptop into a very heavy and very expensive flying projectile. If it's in the front seat, it could end up being smashed to smithereens; if it's in a back seat, you could end up with several kilograms of plastic and metal hitting you in the back of the head.

Thankfully, injuries from flying laptops are rare, but injuries to laptops are all too common. For everyday travel we'd recommend investing in a good, sturdy laptop case to protect your computer from hard knocks. Such cases aren't expensive, and you'll find that firms such as Targus (**www.targus.com**) make cases to suit every budget from basic cases to air-filled, shock-absorbing, side-impact-deflecting models that could probably withstand a nuclear war. No matter how tough your case, though, always take your laptop as hand luggage when you fly. Your case might be able to withstand a nuclear war, but it probably can't withstand the trials of baggage handling.

Of course, it's possible to damage your computer without leaving the house. Spilling cola or coffee on a keyboard can ruin it, and if the keyboard is part of your laptop computer then the liquid could cause serious – and expensive – damage to the computer itself. Rather than bring food and drink into your office, it's a better idea to get up and go to the kitchen instead. Not only does that remove the risk of spillages, but the thirst or hunger pangs will encourage you to take a break from the computer!

Children and animals can be a risk, too: inquisitive toddlers might tug on trailing cables or try to put things in sockets, while a pet might decide that one of your gadgets is an exciting new toy. We lost an expensive mobile phone for that very reason last week when our puppy decided that the phone was an interactive chew toy. Any steps you can take to minimise such risks, from using cable ties to fitting baby gates or locking the office door when you're not using it, can minimise the risk to your equipment and, of course, the risk of injury to children or pets.

Security products such as Kensington's Microsaver are a very effective way to prevent your computer from being stolen, and there are versions for both laptop and desktop PCs.

Data security and disaster recovery

There are two kinds of data to worry about: the data on your computer and the data you keep on paper. If someone got their hands on your paper documents, could they cause trouble for you, your employer or your clients? If the answer is yes, invest in a sturdy, lockable filing cabinet and consider using a document shredder to destroy any sensitive documents you don't intend to keep. The risk of someone raking through your dustbin to steal data is very small, but as shredders and locking file cabinets aren't expensive they may be worthwhile investments.

Computer-data security is a bit more complicated. You need to secure your data in two ways: by stopping it falling into the wrong hands and by preventing it from becoming damaged. Data security is particularly important if you're handling personal data such as databases of customers or other confidential data. Under

The UK Information Commissioner provides lots of information on the Data Protection Act, including your responsibilities for protecting confidential information and whether you may be exempt from the law.

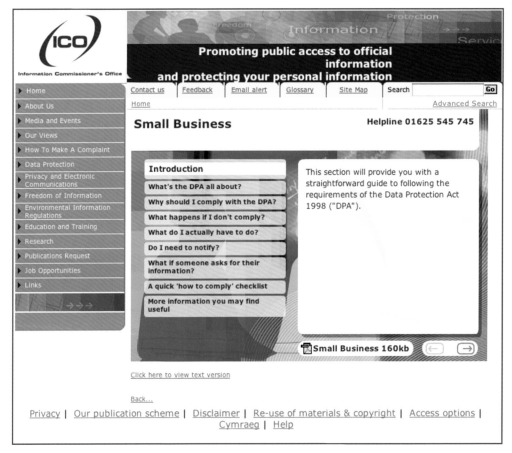

the Data Protection Act you must ensure that the data you hold is only kept for as long as necessary, and that the data you hold is stored securely. Not all data is covered by the Data Protection Act, though: for example if you're only keeping records of contacts for marketing purposes, you're probably exempt from the Act. You can find out full details from the Information Commissioner on 01625 545 745 or by visiting **www.ico.gov.uk**.

Ensuring your data doesn't fall into the wrong hands

As we discovered in Part 2 of this manual, if you use a wireless network it's important to enable the security features to stop others from getting access to your system, and it's a good idea to use firewall software to protect you against security risks when you use the internet. If the information you're dealing with is particularly sensitive, consider the use of encryption software such as Cryptainer LE (**www.cypherix.co.uk**): this scrambles your documents or messages using an almost unbreakable code, and the only way to unscramble them again is to enter the correct password. For really sensitive data, it's also sensible to securely wipe your hard disk – most security suites include a secure deletion tool – if you're selling or giving away an old PC.

While there are security risks online and with wireless networks, by far the biggest security risk is from losing or misplacing a computer. Around 100,000 laptops get damaged in the UK every year, and a further 67,000 are stolen; in just six months in London during 2004, people left 63,135 mobile phones, 5,838 Pocket PCs and 4,973 laptops in the back of taxis. If you're lucky, a stolen laptop will be wiped and re-sold; if you're unlucky, criminals could poke around your files and discover important data such as your online banking details or your top-secret client files. You should never store such data on your computer, or on gadgets such as your mobile phone, unless you use encryption software that makes it impossible for others to access it. Losing your hardware's bad enough, but letting criminals clean out your business's bank account is even worse.

Ensuring damaged data doesn't mean disaster

Computers are generally very reliable, but there are a number of potential problems that could destroy your valuable data. Over the years we've experienced all of the following:

- *Accidentally overwriting important documents with blank ones*
- *Accidentally deleting entire folders full of important files*
- *Moving files to a CD to free up hard disk space – and then losing the CD*

- *Upgrading the operating system and choosing the 'clean install' option by mistake, erasing the entire hard disk*
- *Installing a software update that corrupts important data*
- *Spikes in the power supply causing a crash and corrupting data*
- *Complete and catastrophic hardware failure*

You can protect against some of these problems – using a surge protector between the mains electricity and your computer can prevent power spikes, while being really careful can prevent the accidental overwriting or erasing of documents – but not all of them. And they aren't the only potential problems. Every year data recovery firm OnTrack (**www.ontrack.com**) compiles its Top Ten Computer Disasters, and in recent years the list has included these catastrophes:

- *The man who accidentally deleted every single digital photo of his new-born baby*
- *The woman who tripped and dropped a heavy pot on her computer, smashing it to smithereens*
- *The man who attempted to fix a hard disk failure by taking his computer apart, and realised halfway through that he had no idea what he was doing*
- *The dog that thought a USB flash drive was a tasty toy, and chewed it to bits*
- *The man whose laptop mysteriously crashed all the time, because – as he eventually discovered – his nephew would repeatedly punch it whenever it ran slowly*
- *The medical company worker who spent several days processing 1,200 customer billing entries, and then lost the lot when lightning struck the transformer next to the building*
- *The buildings expert who took his laptop with him to a construction site and watched in horror as a reinforced steel beam fell on it*
- *The executive who placed her laptop on the roof of her car while she opened the car door. Distracted, she forgot about it – and when she put the car in gear, the laptop fell off the roof and landed on the ground. None the wiser, the executive promptly reversed over it*
- *The writer who got so fed up with her computer, she attacked it with a hammer*
- *The company director who tried to catch up on work while having a bath, and dropped his laptop in the water*
- *The man on a moped whose laptop fell from his bag as he went round a corner. It fell under the wheels of a lorry*

How an uninterruptible power supply can protect you from power cuts

Power problems can be bad for your data in two ways: spikes in the electricity supply could damage your data or even damage your hardware, and a power cut when you're in the middle of something important could mean losing a morning's work. You can prevent the former by using an extension lead that includes surge protection, but of course it's impossible to prevent power cuts – unless you buy an uninterruptible power supply, or UPS for short.

A UPS is essentially a big battery pack that sits between your PC and the mains supply. When the power's running normally the UPS filters out surges and other potential power problems, but if the power fails the batteries kick in and you can keep working – although a typical UPS only gives you a few minutes of power, which is long enough to save your files and shut down your computer but not long enough to do any additional work. You can buy a UPS for less than £100.

Of course, few of these things are likely to happen to you (although we're sure we're not the only ones who've felt like attacking our computers with a hammer from time to time) and the reason OnTrack publishes the top ten is because, in every case, the firm successfully recovered the customer's data. They'd hardly publish a list of their top ten failures, after all. However, data recovery costs money and takes time. Had the unfortunate owners made backup copies of all their important files, they could have used those backups on another computer and returned to work almost immediately – without losing a single document.

As you can see from the table of backup methods, there are a number of ways to make backups and the method you choose depends on your particular requirements. However, the principles are the same no matter what method you choose: if you need it, back it up – and back it up regularly. That means all your important documents, but also address books, spreadsheets, accounting records or any other files on which you depend.

In some cases, it's also a good idea to have a paper copy of key data, so for example if you're self-employed and use an Excel spreadsheet to track your income, expenditure and tax liability then it's worth taking a printout as well as making regular backups. If you're exceptionally unlucky and disaster strikes not just your computer but your backup too, you've still got the printed copy to refer to.

Backup methods: the good, the bad and the ugly

The method	The good	The bad	The ugly
Backing up to your own computer	It's very fast and very easy; it protects you against accidental deletion or damage to key files; if you use Windows XP, the software – System Restore – is already in your computer	Your backup is on the same computer as the original files	Theft, hardware failure or user error could mean you'll lose the originals and the backup too
Backing up to another computer	You don't need any additional hardware other than a network cable	You'll need to get to grips with basic computer networking. It's not too difficult, but it's a bit time consuming	You need to have a second computer – which is an expensive option if it's only being used for backups
Backing up using floppy disks	Floppy disks are exceptionally cheap	Floppy disks have a tiny storage capacity; backing up even a few files is painfully slow	Most modern PCs don't come with floppy disk drives; disks can be wiped by magnetic fields
Backing up to CDs or DVDs	Discs are very cheap; one CD is the equivalent of hundreds of floppies, and DVDs are bigger still	You might need extra software; for big backups on CD, you'll still need lots of blank discs	Discs are easily scratched, and there are concerns over their longevity – especially with cheaper products
Backing up to an external hard disk	Massive storage capacities and very fast data transfer speeds mean it's the fastest way to make big backups	If there's a disaster in your house, the external hard disk could be affected too	A hard disk is much more expensive than a 10-pack of blank CDs
Backing up to an internet storage site, or your own web space	Your backup is stored far, far away; it's relatively easy to do; there are lots of firms offering online backup, many of them for little or no money	It's pointless if you don't have a broadband connection; even then, it's often painfully slow; there are potential security risks too	If your broadband connection has usage limits, backing up could exceed them; are you confident the internet company will stay in business?
Making printed copies of important data	It's quick, cheap and easy, and you don't need special tools to do it	Keeping printouts isn't practical if you have huge quantities of data	If the original files get damaged, you'll need to type it all back in again
Not backing up at all	Requires no time, money or hardware	You don't have a backup at all; you're tempting fate	Disaster **will** strike, and when it does you'll lose everything

How often should you make a backup?

You should always make a backup before doing anything big, such as installing a software upgrade, adding new hardware or taking your laptop on a business trip – or after anything big, such as when you complete a large project or reach the end of a quarter or financial year. In addition, you should make regular backups too.

The frequency of your backups depends on how much you use your computer and what type of backups you prefer to make, so for example if you've got an external hard disk there's no reason why you couldn't make a new backup every day (the software that comes with the disk can usually do it for you: just tell it when you want it to backup your system and it takes care of the rest) – and if you spend all day every day entering data or creating things on your computer, then a daily backup would be a very good idea. On the other hand if you spend most of your time on the phone, only use the computer for basic record keeping and backup your files to CDs, a daily backup would be unnecessary and far too time-consuming.

There's no right or wrong backup method and there's no law that says you must backup daily, weekly or monthly, but whatever method you choose and whatever frequency you decide upon, it's important to stick to a routine – so if you plan to backup weekly, make sure you do and that you keep the backups somewhere safe. You can be confident that if you skip a backup or misplace your CDs, that's when disaster will strike.

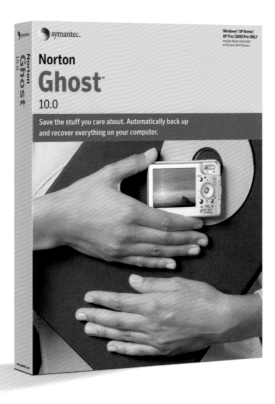

Programs such as Symantec's Norton Ghost (**www.symantec.co.uk/product**) are designed to backup important files – and to recover them if things go wrong.

7

PART **7**

Appendices

PART

Appendix 1:
Money, money, money

When it comes to financial things, there's good news and bad news for homeworkers. The good news is that you can often claim expenses – including a proportion of your heating and electricity bills – against tax, but the bad news is that you need to think about insurance and, in some cases, rates too.

Homeworking and the taxman

When you work from home you should expect your domestic bills to increase. You'll use more electricity because you're running computers and other office equipment, and in winter you'll need to light your work area during office hours. You'll use more gas, because you'll have the central heating on more often, and if your water supply is metered you'll probably notice a slight increase in your water bills too.

If you're employed by a company, it's possible to claim a proportion of these expenses against your tax bill, but HM Revenue & Customs would rather you didn't: in 2005, it capped the tax relief for phone calls, electricity, gas and water charges at just £2 per week for employed homeworkers. It also stated that you could only claim tax relief on these expenses 'if no such appropriate facilities are available to the employee on the employer's premises' and that 'at no time before or after the contract is drawn up is the employee able to choose between working at the employer's premises or elsewhere'. In other words, unless you're forced to work from home against your will then you shouldn't try to claim expenses against your tax bill.

To be fair, the government does have a point. If you work from home, you're saving your employer money: the more homeworkers a firm has, the less it needs to spend on premises, power and water. Why should the firm keep those savings and expect the taxman to cover your costs? In most cases, if you work from home it's up to the employer to reimburse you for any extra bills – and you'll often find that the firm won't, because you no longer need to pay travel costs or other expenses.

If you're self-employed, things are more cheerful. You can claim a proportion of your home bills – heating, power, electricity and even rent – against tax, provided that you can demonstrate that your home office is only used for business purposes (so if your office is in a corner of the bedroom, you won't be able to argue that the room is solely used for work!). The easiest way to work out what you're entitled to is by square footage, so for example if your office takes up 10% of the overall square footage of your home, then you'd claim 10% of the electricity, gas and water bills.

Be very careful when you claim home expenses against tax, though: if you claim a proportion of your home expenses, you might find that you're liable for Capital Gains Tax when you sell your home. This is a tax on business profits, and the bills can be scary. We'd strongly advise speaking to an experienced accountant about such issues before you start filling out tax returns.

In addition to home expenses, self-employed people can claim any legitimate business expense – but the things you claim for can't be used for personal matters. For example, if you use the same phone for home and business use, you can't claim for the whole phone bill; if you travel on business but stay with friends, the taxman sees that as a personal trip, not a business one. Unfortunately you can't claim for daily lunches or a new dressing gown, but you can claim depreciation on the costs of office equipment and computers, on the cost of business-related finance (such as business banking costs, interest on finance deals and so on) and on other expenses such as business-related mileage.

You'll find that it makes life much easier if you keep your personal life and business life separate, so for example we'd recommend a separate business bank account, a separate business telephone line and so on. We'd also recommend hiring an accountant: totting up your tax bill each year shouldn't cost more than around £300 for a basic service, and you'll often find that your accountant will suggest ways to reduce your tax bill that more than justify the cost of hiring him or her.

You can also get advice from another source: the taxman. Don't let their scary reputation put you off: HM Revenue & Customs employees are very helpful, particularly if you're looking for advice on self-employment. You'll find a large range of factsheets

HM Revenue & Customs produces lots of advice for self-employed people, including the award-winning 'Working for yourself' guide. Download it from **www.hmrc.gov.uk/startingup**.

and guides on the HM Revenue & Customs site (**www.hmrc.gov.uk**), or you can call the Self Assessment helpline on 0845 9000 444.

Paying your tax bill

When you're in full-time employment, tax is simple: your employer works out what you need to pay, deducts it from your wages, and gives the money directly to the taxman. However if you're self-employed it's a bit more complicated than that. Sorting out your tax bill is entirely your responsibility.

Self-employed people pay several kinds of taxes, and the main ones are National Insurance contributions and Income Tax. If you're doing exceptionally well, you'll also pay Value Added Tax (VAT) – but you'll need a turnover of at least £60,000 per year before you need to worry about that.

If you're self-employed you'll pay two kinds of National Insurance contributions: Class 2 contributions and Class 4 contributions. Class 2 contributions are set at a standard weekly rate (currently £2.10) and paid via direct debit; Class 4 contributions are a tax on profits, and you pay them at the same time as you pay your income tax bill. The rate for Class 4 contributions is currently 8% on profits between £5,035 and £33,540 per year, plus 1% on profits above £33,540.

As with Class 4 contributions, Income Tax is paid on profits – the figure you're left with when you deduct business expenses from your income. All taxpayers have a tax-free allowance, and once your profits exceed this figure you'll pay income tax on the lot. Income tax is levied on taxable profits, which are:

What you earned during the tax year
Minus your legitimate business expenses for that year
Minus your personal tax allowance (currently £5,035)

For example, if you earned £20,000 and had £3,000 in expenses, your profit would be £17,000 – but your taxable profit would be £11,965. This is the figure you'd use to work out how much tax you need to pay.

There are three rates of income tax: the starting rate, the basic rate and the higher rate. These work as follows (all figures are for the 2006/2007 tax year):

Starting rate	10% on the first £2,090 of taxable profits
Basic rate	22% on taxable profits from £2,090 to £32,400
Higher rate	40% on taxable profits from £32,400 upwards

Remember, Class 4 National Insurance applies too: it's a further 8% of your taxable profits.

The tax year ends in the first week of April, and you've got until the end of September to submit your tax return. You then pay the tax in two instalments: at the end of January, and at the end of July. If you don't submit your tax return on time or, worse, don't pay your tax in time, you'll be charged penalty fees and interest on any outstanding tax.

Keeping records

As you'd expect, the taxman expects to see evidence of your expenses – and you need to keep your records available for inspection for five years after the tax return deadline. According to HM Revenue & Customs, these are the records you must keep:

- *Records of all sales and business receipts*
- *Additional records such as bank statements and paying-in slips*
- *Receipts for all purchases and other expenses 'unless the amounts are very small'*
- *Records of all purchases and sales of business assets*
- *Records of all sums taken out of the business bank account*
- *Records of all amounts paid into the business from personal funds*

For full details of record-keeping rules and regulations, download leaflet SA/BK4 (**www.hmrc.gov.uk/pdfs/sabk4.htm**) from the HM Revenue & Customs website.

Homeworking and the local council

Councils levy two kinds of taxes on property: Council Tax for residential property and business rates for business properties. So which should you be paying? In the majority of cases, you won't be liable for business rates – but it's important to check.

If your home office is little more than a desk, you won't have to pay business rates. However, depending on the council you might have to pay business rates if you've converted the garage into business premises or if you regularly meet clients in your home. However, for rates purposes your work area would need to be used entirely for commercial purposes, so for example if you use the garage as an office but also use it to store your lawnmower then you could argue that you should not pay business rates.

Some of the confusion over business rates for homeworkers was addressed in 2004, when Eileen Tully appealed to the Lands Tribunal after her local council demanded that she pay business rates. Tully worked from a bedroom, and the Lands Tribunal judged that she did not need to pay business rates for such homeworking. However, as *The Observer*'s Andrew Bibby drily noted when he reported the verdict:

Mrs Tully's spare room was reclassified as business premises only because she had herself, perhaps rather unwisely, contacted the district valuer to point out that she was using a bedroom as an office and to ask for a council tax reduction. Without that, it is highly unlikely that any authority would have been aware of her move to home-working. It is hard to avoid the conclusion that the wisest course for many people beginning working from home may simply be: keep it quiet.

Beware of planning regulations and other restrictions too. Some homes have restrictions in their lease, rental agreement or mortgage that prohibit homeworking, and some homeworking situations may require planning permission from the local council. If you intend to advertise your business by putting a sign in the garden, if you carry out structural alterations such as turning a garage into an office or if your business will involve other individuals (employees or clients) then the council may deem such changes a 'material change of use', for which you'll need planning permission. The idea behind such permission is to prevent companies from turning residential premises into office blocks, and while change of use regulations won't affect most homeworkers it's definitely worth checking with the council if you're unsure.

Safe as houses

Health and safety is essential in any workplace, and that includes your home. It's a very good idea to carry out a risk assessment, which is when you identify any potential hazards in your working area. According to Business Link, the advice centre for small businesses, possible homeworking hazards include:

The Health and Safety Executive publishes lots of guidance for homeworkers, including this leaflet. You can download it free from **www.hse.gov.uk/pubns/ indg226.pdf**.

- *Work equipment including electrical appliances*
- *Your workstation setup*
- *Handling heavy objects*
- *Hazardous substances and materials*
- *Psychological hazards, such as stress and loneliness*
- *Fire, slips, trips and falls*
- *Excessive noise or vibration*

One of the most common hazards for homeworkers is injury from equipment, such as repetitive strain injury from using computers. We'll take a detailed look at these risks – and how to prevent them – in Appendix 3.

When you consider workplace risks, it's important not just to think about your own safety, but that of others such as family members. Once you've done that, you need to decide what action – if any – you need to take to minimise the risks to you and to anyone else who shares or visits your home.

Essential insurance

More and more home insurance policies automatically cover you for home office equipment, but it's important to make sure. For

Although many insurance policies cover home office equipment, the cover might not be adequate for your needs. It's worth considering dedicated business insurance, particularly if you'll be working from multiple locations.

example, if you get home insurance from Direct Line you get £5,000 of cover for your home office equipment – but your work must be 'confined to routine paperwork and telephone calls or registered childminding'. If you do other kinds of work, you aren't covered.

Some firms provide cover for laptops, which can be useful if you regularly travel away from home. Again, watch the terms and conditions: Cornhill Direct's home insurance policy does indeed cover laptops, but only if they're for personal, not business, use. If you want to cover your business laptop, you'll need to ask for, and pay for, the extra Home Worker cover.

If you're buying expensive office equipment, make sure that the insurer provides sufficient cover for each item. For example, the Royal Bank of Scotland provides £5,000 of cover for home office equipment, but it has a per-item limit of £1,500 for any items not specifically named in your policy documents. Similarly More Than covers business equipment up to £7,500, but again its per-item limit is £1,500 – and there's a limit of £1,000 for items stolen from a motor vehicle.

Other exclusions are potentially more serious. In the case of More Than's home insurance, there's a very big exclusion under 'Theft or attempted theft': you're not covered 'if your home is used to receive visitors in connection with your business operating from your home'. Most insurers have similar exclusions, which is why it's so important to read the small print carefully – or you could end up with a policy that won't pay out if disaster strikes.

Liability insurance

In addition to the usual theft and accident insurance, some businesses need other kinds of insurance too. If you have clients visiting you at home, then Public Liability Insurance is a good idea; and if you make products, then Product Liability Insurance would be sensible. If you intend to employ people who aren't your immediate family then you'll need Employers' Liability Insurance too.

Employers' Liability Insurance is compulsory for any firm with more than one employee (excepting immediate family members, such as husband and wife partnerships), and you can be fined up to £2,500 for every day you don't have it. ELI provides insurance against claims from employees who fell ill or became injured in your workplace through errors or negligence on your part.

Public Liability Insurance is optional, but worth considering if you'll be letting clients or customers visit your office. The insurance protects you from potentially expensive claims, such as someone tripping over a cable in your office and incurring a serious injury.

Product Liability Insurance is less common and is only worth considering if you manufacture goods. It protects you in the event that your product damages property or causes injury to someone.

Appendix 2: Staying sane

One of the great ironies of homeworking is that the two biggest problems you'll face couldn't be more different. The first big problem is too much contact with other people, and the second is lack of contact with other people. When you first work from home, it's often hard to convince others that you're actually working and that you need to be left alone – and at the same time, the lack of office banter can make you feel very isolated. In this section we'll take an in-depth look at the potential problems and we'll discover how you can address them.

The 'work' bit of homeworking

One thing many people seem to have problems understanding is that just because you're at home, it doesn't mean you're constantly available. Friends pop round for a chat on their day off and spend the entire afternoon drinking your tea; relatives make long phone calls at the most inconvenient times; and you'll get lots of requests to feed dogs, pick up parcels, pop round to the shops, and so on.

According to a recent survey of homeworkers by Norwich Union, the top two distractions for homeworkers are personal visitors during office hours and friends phoning for a gossip, with 62% of homeworkers claiming that friends and family thought their day involved lounging around on sofas, watching daytime television – but the reality is that a typical homeworker does a 45-hour week, compared to the UK average of a 39-hour week. As the survey noted, 'nine out of ten people working from home say they made the change for a more flexible lifestyle or to spend time with their family, but the majority admit they work longer hours at home than their office counterparts'.

The best way to address the problem of interruptions is to nip it in the bud. If friends pop round, explain that it's great to see them but you can only spare a few minutes; if you're too busy to take a call, say so at the outset and arrange to call back at a time that suits you better; and if you're bombarded with requests, learn to say no. If you establish ground rules and stick to them, people will quickly get the message and leave you in peace to get on with your work.

If you share your home with others – flatmates, family members or pets – it's a very good idea to have a dedicated, separate working area instead of a corner of a room that's in constant use. Family members watching TV, flatmates making telephone calls or pets demanding attention are all surprisingly disruptive, and you'll find that if you can go somewhere else and shut the door, your productivity will rocket.

Not all interruptions come from others, though. It's important to keep yourself focused, too – and if a March 2006 survey by

technology firm SonicWall is any indication, not all homeworkers are good doing that. 28 per cent of homeworkers surveyed admitted that they watched TV during working hours, while a further 21 per cent admitted to sneaky daytime naps. And of course the internet is a great timewaster, too. The UK's Cranfield School of Management estimates that employees of small businesses waste one day per week on non-work email and web browsing, and we suspect that some homeworkers waste even more time on non-work browsing.

One of the easiest ways to stay focused on your work is to get into a routine. Everybody will have a different routine but, for example, you could deal with personal emails before starting work in the morning and then ignore personal messages until lunchtime, or you might save your personal web browsing for tea breaks. If you feel that you could do with more help staying focused and managing your time more effectively, you'll find hundreds of 'life hacks' – productivity tips – at the excellent Lifehacker.com (**www.lifehacker.com**) – but don't look at it if you can't spare the time!

Avoiding isolation

Working from home can be isolating, and many people suffer from 'cabin fever' – a feeling of claustrophobia from staring at the same four walls every day. The Norwich Union survey of homeworkers came up with the following suggestions for happy homeworking:

- *Establish a daily routine. Create a realistic routine to help you stay focused and motivated and allow time for non-work breaks too.*
- *Create a dedicated work area. Whether it's a separate room, desk or work surface, a dedicated workspace will help make the switch to 'home mode'.*

Visits from friends or family members can make homeworking less isolating, but it's important to set ground rules too: people need to realise that you can't always spare time during your working day.

- *Build a support network. Maintain and build business contacts that can offer you advice and keep you abreast of market trends and industry news. They may also be able to pass on all-important new business leads.*
- *Learn how to deal with interruptions. Establish ground rules for other household members and make it clear that when you are at your desk you are not to be disturbed.*
- *Get out of the house. To ward off cabin fever, ensure you schedule appointments, both business and social, away from your home.*

We'd add five more suggestions:
- *Make room in your life for your life. It's easy to fall into the trap of working long hours, but if you take time out to relax then you'll be happier and more productive, and considerably more popular with your partner, your friends and your family. Wherever possible, avoid working evenings and weekends unless the future of your business or this month's mortgage payment absolutely depends on it – and take holidays!*
- *Remember that you're still at work. It's tempting to catch up on odd jobs around the home or to take care of household chores, and there's nothing wrong with doing either – provided you're not contracted to work specific hours and that they don't get in the way of your work. DIY in particular is a notorious 'time thief': the job that you think will only take a few minutes can easily turn into an all-day epic requiring repeated trips to B&Q and, if you're unlucky, antiseptic and plasters.*
- *Look after yourself. Sitting at a desk all day isn't the greatest way to stay in shape, so it's important to eat healthily and get lots of exercise – whether that's going to the gym, walking the dog or going for a bike ride. Exercise doesn't just help you stay in shape: it helps you stay alert and does wonders for your mood, too.*
- *Expand your social circle. There are lots of opportunities to interact with others, not just in the business world but in your local community too. If you're suffering from cabin fever, you could always join a dance class, do some volunteer work or anything else that takes you out of the house and into something that interests you.*
- *Enjoy yourself. One of the great advantages of homeworking is that there's nobody breathing down your neck, so if you want to sit around in a tatty dressing-gown while eating digestives and listening to heavy metal then go right ahead. According to Norwich Union's survey, one in 10 homeworkers conducts business in their pyjamas while more than one third have conducted important business calls while cuddling partners, children or pets; more worryingly, SonicWall's survey found that 12 per cent of male homeworkers and 7 per cent of female homeworkers are sitting naked at the keyboard. Then again, that survey was in California. We suspect the numbers would be considerably lower for homeworkers in northern Scotland.*

Appendix 3: Ergonomics

Homeworking has many benefits, but there's one big drawback. In an office environment your employer needs to make sure you're safe, but at home it's up to you. If you'll be using a computer for long periods, it's important to know about repetitive strain injury (RSI) – and to take steps to avoid it.

RSI isn't a disease. Rather, it's a catch-all term for lots of different injuries: carpal tunnel syndrome, writers' cramp, tennis elbow, trigger finger, vibration white finger, tendinitis, frozen shoulder, and so on. Although the injuries have different symptoms, they're all very painful and they all have the same common cause: they're the result of doing the same thing over and over again for long periods of time, often with bad posture.

According to the TUC, 1 in 50 UK workers suffer from RSI, and six people in the UK leave their jobs because of RSI every day. Sixty per cent of Swedish office workers have RSI symptoms, as do 60 per cent of Australian children who use laptops at school and 40 per cent of Dutch university students. A recent survey by the Health and Safety Executive found that 506,000 UK workers suffered from a work-related upper limb or neck disorder, and that figure may be the tip of a very painful iceberg.

Homeworkers are particularly prone to RSI, because they tend to work for long hours without breaks – and because they don't have Health and Safety officers peering over their shoulder to make sure they're OK. So what causes RSI – and more importantly, what can you do to prevent it?

Risky business

RSI is often seen as the result of too much typing, but using a keyboard and mouse doesn't mean you'll suffer an injury. There are five key causes of RSI: repetitive movements, forceful movements, physical stresses, static or uncomfortable posture, and vibration.

These five factors explain why some computer users develop RSI, while other users – who may work in the same location, doing the same job – remain pain-free. Repeating the same movements again and again for long periods of time is certainly a risk factor, but if you also hit the computer keys with excessive force and maintain the same posture for long periods of time without a break – especially if that posture is bad posture – then your risk of RSI increases dramatically.

Stress is a factor, too. People who work in high-pressure environments with little job security may take fewer breaks and work longer hours than people with less stressful jobs; the long hours culture is also endemic among self-employed people and people on short-term or fixed-term contracts, who may eschew breaks and work through the night in order to meet deadlines.

Another reason why these high-pressure environments are risky is that they often involve little variety. Someone employed to do data entry or programming will spend most, if not all, of their working hours using a computer, whereas someone in an administrative job may alternate between computer work, paperwork, telephone calls and so on.

One of the key reasons why some people contract RSI and others don't is posture. Bad posture can be the result of inadequate ergonomics, such as an uncomfortable chair and a desk that's too high, or it can be self-inflicted: for example, many people rest the weight of their arm on the heel of their hand while using the mouse, a habit that can easily lead to crippling pain. In some cases it's both: users who are unaware of the risk of RSI may not realise that their working environment is dangerous. We've seen computer setups that beggar belief: for example, a designer in a DIY firm whose computer monitor was mounted on the wall, two feet above head height and at an angle of 45 degrees from the keyboard. Even though computer use was only a small part of that person's job, the ridiculous placement of computer equipment was already causing severe neck and shoulder pains.

Correct posture is all about right angles. Your feet should be flat on the floor, with your calves vertical and your thighs horizontal; your back should be upright and your monitor placed directly in front of you with the top of the screen at head height. Your arms should also be at right angles: your upper arms vertical, and your forearms horizontal. Resting your wrists on the desk as you type is a no-no, and some ergonomics experts suggest that the use of wrist wrests is equally dangerous.

You can make your working environment more ergonomic by thinking about angles. When you type, your forearms should be horizontal and your upper arms vertical, your thighs horizontal and your calves vertical.

If you'll be using a laptop for long periods, it's a good idea to use a separate keyboard and mouse together with a laptop stand such as Griffin's iCurve (**www.griffintechnology.com/products/icurve**).

Correct posture is easy enough with a desktop, but what about laptops? Their design means that correct posture is almost impossible – if the screen is at the right height, the typing position is abysmal – so if you intend to use a laptop for long periods, it's sensible to put it on a stand and use a separate keyboard and mouse.

You should also pay close attention to your working environment to identify and address any potential dangers. For example if you have to refer to printed documentation, constantly shifting your gaze from monitor to desk can cause neck and shoulder strain – strain that can be prevented with a £5 document holder.

Finally, you should take lots of breaks. No matter how safe your working environment, long periods of uninterrupted computer use can still cause damage. Taking a few quick breaks during each hour of computer use can dramatically reduce this damage, which means you're less likely to end up taking a permanent break from computer work.

Healing hands: what to do if you contract RSI

RSI is often viewed as incurable, but treatment – and changing your behaviour – can reduce the symptoms. Avoiding the tasks that caused your RSI in the first place – whether that's computer work, tennis or gardening – is sensible, and you should avoid using painkillers to mask the pain while you keep working. If you do that, you're continuing to damage your body and make your RSI even worse – and when the painkillers wear off, you'll be in agony.

If you suspect that you have RSI, the first thing to do is to get professional medical advice. Your GP may be able to help, and he or she could refer you to a sports injury specialist (many sportsmen and women contract RSI). Some sufferers report good results from supplements such as Glucosamine Sulphate, others from acupuncture, still others from deep massage. Some sufferers find that alternative therapies such as the Bowen Technique helps although, of course, other sufferers feel that such treatments were expensive and unsuccessful.

We've interviewed many RSI sufferers, and they tell us that two treatments seem to be particularly effective: physiotherapy and the Alexander Technique. Sufferers report that physiotherapists specialising in sports injuries, in particular, can make a real difference and you'll often find such therapists working in, affiliated to or advertising in local health clubs.

The Alexander Technique is more controversial: some sufferers dismiss it as 'tree-hugging mumbo-jumbo' while others sing its praises from the rooftops. The Technique focuses on improving posture and reducing stress, and its adherents – of whom there are many – point out that poor posture and excessive stress are contributing factors in many cases of RSI. More information and local contact details are available from the Society of Teachers of the Alexander Technique website (**www.stat.org.uk**).

It's important to take RSI seriously: if you get aches and pains when you work, don't discount them – and don't simply take painkillers and carry on working. If your working area follows ergonomic principles, you take lots of breaks and you don't work too long hours, RSI is entirely avoidable – and if you do get it, it's manageable. If you have even the slightest cause for concern, speak to your GP.

Don't ignore aches and pains: if you're sore after using your PC, it's a warning sign that either your posture or your working environment is putting you at risk of RSI.

Index

Acknowledgments:
Grateful thanks to Iain Maclean for the product
photography, Kyle MacRae for his help and to Dell for
providing us with the equipment.

Authors	**Gary Marshall** **and Kyle MacRae**
Copy Editor	**Shena Deuchars**
Page build	**James Robertson**
Index	**Nigel d'Auvergne**
Project Manager	**Louise McIntyre**